20 YEARS OF SALT
(In a 10-Pound Bag)

HARRY SALTZGAVER

outskirtspress
DENVER, COLORADO

The opinions expressed in this manuscript are solely the opinions of the author and do not represent the opinions or thoughts of the publisher. The author has represented and warranted full ownership and/or legal right to publish all the materials in this book.

20 Years Of Salt
(In A 10-Pound Bag)
All Rights Reserved.
Copyright © 2013 Harry Saltzgaver
v2.0

This book may not be reproduced, transmitted, or stored in whole or in part by any means, including graphic, electronic, or mechanical without the express written consent of the publisher except in the case of brief quotations embodied in critical articles and reviews.

Outskirts Press, Inc.
http://www.outskirtspress.com

ISBN: 978-1-4787-1104-9

Outskirts Press and the "OP" logo are trademarks belonging to Outskirts Press, Inc.

PRINTED IN THE UNITED STATES OF AMERICA

Contents

Acknowledgments i

Introduction iii

Part ONE
    The Animal Stories 1

Part TWO
    Stories In The News 37

Part THREE
    About The Life I Lead 89

Part FOUR
    All About Long Beach 167

Part FIVE
    The Spirit Of Faith 223

Part SIX
    One More For Good Measure 279

Acknowledgments

Thanks are in order for my various publishers during my years with Gazette Newspapers, but most especially for Fran and John Blowitz, the couple who had confidence in me and the same philosophy about community newspapers as mine.

Special thanks also to Simon Grieve, the publisher for the last five years of my first two decades as the executive editor of those publications. As he says, we make a pretty good team.

And thanks to my family members, who put up with me taking their names in vain in print, and with the crazy hours I spend in this profession and town I love.

Finally, thanks to all the readers who have followed me and 'A Pinch Of Salt" over the years, allowing me to share and grow. There wouldn't be a reason to do it at all if it wasn't for you.

Harry Saltzgaver
Jan. 30, 2013

All columns in this book first appeared in the print edition of the Grunion Gazette, and are reprinted here with permission. Cover design by Terri Lancaster.

Introduction

Having your own column means, for most newspaper types, getting to the top of the heap.

For a good century now, columnists have been the stars of the newspaper business. Sure, there have been the Woodwards and the Bernsteins (and they are great), but newspapers often tied their personality, their identity, to their columnists.

Think about the Los Angeles Times' sports page. Do you remember the game stories? Of course not. You think Jim Murray.

Think Chicago. Doesn't matter whether you think of a newspaper, you think Royko.

So naturally, I wanted to be a columnist. But the superstar column spots are few and far between, and I seemed to have a talent for reporting the news, so I got into the business where I could.

By the time I got to Long Beach, I had had the opportunity to exercise my column muscles on occasion. But the Gazette offered me the chance to write a column on a regular basis.

From the beginning, the idea behind "A Pinch Of Salt" was to put a human face on the paper. That didn't mean writing about my personal life every week – far from it. It meant offering opinions, admitting mistakes, trying to explain positions – and writing about my personal life.

Twenty years later, I think for the most part the column has done its job. I know that when I'm out in public, people talk more about my family, my dogs and my struggles at being a home handyman than they do about the news of the day (although fortunately, there's plenty of that, as well).

I could think of no better way to celebrate my 20th anniversary than to compile what I thought were the best Pinches to have appeared during that time. I quickly discovered that defining what was "best" might be a tougher job than writing them in the first place.

So I decided to offer a few different types of best. What follows is a selection of opinions about issues facing Long Beach, observations of the life around us, snippets from my personal life, a touch of what I sometimes called guerilla evangelism and some examples of what I hope were humorous columns.

I've tried to provide a paragraph or so of context to try to explain what makes that particular column special to me. But ultimately, they will have to stand on their own, waiting for your judgment.

I hope you enjoy the journey. I certainly did.

Part ONE
The Animal Stories

THE ANIMAL STORIES

I DIDN'T KNOW it at the time, but Hollywood the cat would in many ways define my life in Long Beach for two decades. She'd go through some tough times, not all of her own making (but some that were), but she'd survive. She'd try new things, again with a mix of good and bad results. In sum, it was a good run. And this is how it all began.

May 21, 1992

A cat has invaded my home.

I used to be a dog man. I had dogs as a boy, and a very special canine saw me through college, a marriage and a divorce.

Cats weren't known in my childhood home, and although there has been a cat or two in my adult life, the feline breed never seemed to connect with me.

That, along with just about everything else in my life, has changed in the last year. A little ball of orange energy joined our household last week, and it's already difficult to imagine the place without her.

Actually, the wife and I have been talking about getting a cat since shortly after we were married. Our kids live in Colorado, so a little home companionship seemed like a good idea. But apartments looked like a way of life for us, at least for some time, so a dog was out of the question.

Okay, okay. I'll come clean. A dog never was considered. The wife wanted something that would sit in her lap and purr, and I've never met a dog that would do that.

She (the wife, not the cat) was stubborn, though. She kept swearing she didn't want a kitty. She said it with her mouth, but her eyes said something else.

We stopped by the Long Beach pound a couple of weeks after moving into town. She (the wife again, not the cat) kept putting me off, saying she'd know when "her" kitty came around.

And darned if she wasn't right.

We were driving up Willow after a golf lesson (a whole other column), when she said something about cats. Surprise! The pound was less than a block away.

We spent an hour looking at kittens. There seemed to be hundreds that weekend.

A little orange ball with a crooked tail kept hurtling itself (we didn't know it was a she then) against the bars of the cage, purring like a 747. Wife had said she wanted a white cat, but this one knew how to attract attention.

Now, you have to know that you really have to want a cat to get one from the pound. Except for a couple scruffy old refugees from the alley, all the cats "weren't available." The orange ball and most of its friends couldn't be adopted until 11 a.m. Monday.

Which wouldn't be so bad in itself, but the pound office closes at 4 p.m. More than a little tough for working folks.

But wife wanted one enough that she conned her boss into going with her to the pound on their lunch hour. And Hollywood (that's the cat) found a home.

I must admit, it's a kick watching the little ball do kitten things. And her purr has won me over, even if I do have to play the heavy when she gets on the dining room table. And she (the cat, not the wife) loves to sit on laps.

One little scary note. We thought the cats had five days after they became "available" before the gas chamber beckoned. Turns out the window of life is much shorter.

Hollywood's cage-mate was gone when the wife picked our kitten up. She couldn't bring herself to ask what had happened to the other kitten.

If you've got room in your life for a kitten, consider it. If you've got a cat, get it neutered.

Because cats are a joy – with a home.

ADULTS, PARTICULARLY ADULTS who have children who are not living with them, shouldn't really be allowed to have young pets. There's this thing about anthropomorphism.

It's surprising how many people relate, though. This column seemed to resonate with many readers.

Nov. 6, 1992

It has been a traumatic week at the Saltzgaver household. A family member has gone through major surgery.

Reetz reminded me of a mother bear throughout – fiercely protective. After all, it was her baby they were going to cut.

Hollywood the cat got spayed.

What follows is pretty graphic stuff. Viewer discretion is advised.

Hollywood is about seven months old – we're not exactly sure, since we got her from the animal shelter. But a few weeks ago, she made it abundantly clear she had reached cat puberty.

It's amazing how much noise six pounds of cat can make when she wants something. (Actually, I'm fairly sure she didn't know what it was she wanted – there was a look of frustration on her face that spoke volumes.)

The yowling was bad. But we didn't decide to call the vet until she started dragging herself around on the carpet, trying to scratch the itch she couldn't reach.

Reetz started out all in favor of the procedure. We're a family planning family, after all.

But once the appointment was made, second thoughts began. Reetz swore Hollywood knew what was going on, and wasn't happy about it.

"She's going to hate us," Reetz said. "She's never going to know what it's like to have a man (or Tom, to be exact). She's going to know we did it."

The concerns went deeper. What if something went wrong?

Our vet, Phil Weida, is experienced and one of the best. But there's always a risk.

Would Hollywood still be the playful kitty we had come to know and love? Or would she become The Lump-cat - eating, sleeping and ignoring us?

My son, Alex, didn't help when we called and told him of the plan.

"She won't be doing any of those cute kitty things any more," he said. "Our cat just lays there now."

The night before we took Hollywood to the vet was the worst. We had to take her food away at midnight, so Reetz set the alarm. She started tossing and turning when we turned out the lights, so I foolishly attempted to be amorous.

"How could you?" Reetz said. "Hollywood's listening. And she'll never…"

We made it to the vet without a major battle – mainly because I managed to keep my mouth shut about how it wasn't a big deal. Reetz and I called each other about five times that day, but managed to keep from calling the vet until late afternoon.

We went to pick her up the next day. Hollywood hissed at me when I tried to get her out of the cage. She had an accident in the car on the way home.

She hid when we got her back to the apartment. I swear, it took hours before she would even look at us.

But now, almost a week later, things are pretty much back to normal. Reetz and I still nudge each other and point every time Hollywood plays, but she's back to sitting on our laps and purring – the real reason Reetz wanted a cat to begin with.

I don't think she's going to be a lump, and I suspect she won't miss what she never had. And I have done my social duty by controlling the pet population.

Just one more thing. Anyone out there want to volunteer to take her back to have the stitches out?

I DON'T HAVE the exact statistics, but I'm fairly certain Americans spend more on their pets than any other country. I know I have been unable to say, in nearly 60 years, "That costs too much. Put the animal down."

Here's a case in point.

June 12, 1997

This is the story of the $1,500 cat.

No. I didn't run out and buy a pedigreed Persian. Nor did I find a Siamese on sale.

I'm talking about a runt-of-the-linter, club-tailed, orange tabby rescued from the pound. I've written about her before. She's Hollywood.

Hollywood has had a rough month. She's only a little more than 5 years old – young adulthood in cat years – but apparently her liver decided to shut down.

When she stopped eating a month or so ago, I wasn't overly worried. She'd done it before. I just took it for the cat version of a diet, and she could stand to lose a pound or two (a chip off the old block, as they say).

But when the "diet" persisted for nearly a week, I realized it was time to give Dr. Phil a call. Phil Weida, owner of Blue Cross Dog and Cate Hospital, essentially is the Gazette family veterinarian – and a medic who doesn't give up easily. But more on that later.

Have you ever gone to the doctor for something that seemed minor, only to be told you were in for a hospital stay? That's what happened to Hollywood.

Phil was confident. A few days of fluids and antibiotics, and whatever infection Hollywood had should go away.

But after five days, she appeared no better. In fact, she seemed a little weaker and still wouldn't eat.

"This is a tough one," Phil said. "Let's hang in there, go the full

10 days (the common antibiotic treatment for a liver infection) and see what happens."

I knew we were in trouble when Phil said Hollywood had stopped fighting the technicians during treatments. This is a cat who will fight anyone or anything touching her in the wrong way.

And the moral dilemma began. How much is too much? How badly was she suffering? When do you pull the plug on a pet?

Hollywood couldn't write a living will saying not to take extraordinary measures to keep her alive – like I can, and have. Hollywood couldn't say, "It's not worth it anymore."

I waffled.

Phil stepped in. "Let's give this a shot," he said. "I want to bring a specialist in to do an ultrasound and biopsy. Then we'll know for sure."

That's when the bill topped a grand, by the way. But I said okay.

And sure enough, when the test results came back, we had a confirmed diagnosis – Hollywood had hepatic something-something. It meant that she was essentially digesting her insides, and the only response was to force-feed her through a tube, hoping to reverse the process.

This time, Phil cut my moral debate short.

"We're going to insert the tube and get her eating again," he said. "It's still a very serious situation, but let's give it a shot."

So now I'm filling this syringe you could use on elephants with a gray slime that's full of cat nutrients. Five minutes of pushing the stuff into a tube wrapped around the cat and into her neck like a tracheotomy. We go through the routine three times a day.

Hollywood still isn't out of the woods by any means, but there are some signs of recovery. She's taken to hiding where I can't reach her when it's medicine time, and she actually ate some tuna on her own yesterday.

And she's purring. That purr has kept me from the depths of despair more than once in the last five years. Call me selfish, but I can't give that up just yet.

Long live Hollywood – and the purr.

THE ANIMAL STORIES

TO MY MIND, there are few things as important as choosing a family pet. If, as is the case with most people, you are getting a pet for the children, the chemistry is critical. You are, after all, choosing a member of the family – something you rarely get to do.

We chose well, as you will see.

February 15, 2001

I waited as long as I could. Honest. John and Charlotte started talking about wanting a dog on the odyssey from Colorado, when I first moved the family to Long Beach more than six months ago. The fact our new home had a large, fenced back yard made it difficult to say no.

I managed to dodge the issue through diversion – we have to get the house in order, school's starting, here comes Christmas. Then there was the addition of Erik, our "adopted" grandson. Maria became the primary daycare provider for the little chunk shortly after he was born four months ago.

But things had finally settled down, and Valentine's Day isn't much of a diversion for 11-year-old John (Charlotte, at 14, is too shy to talk about it). The "dog issue" raised its head again.

So Saturday was dog-finding day. Maria and I managed to keep the project a secret until we actually pulled up to the first stop – Belmont Pets, where the dog rescuers were trying to find homes for some puppies. The beaming grins we received were more than ample reward for the secret-keeping.

We didn't find a match there, so it was off to the pound, officially known as the Long Beach Animal Shelter. We spent an interesting two hours there, with the kids bouncing back and forth between several pens, trying to decide who would join our family.

I learned a few things, too, some of which I didn't care for. For example, some dogs are put down (that means killed) the day after they're put up for adoption if no one takes them. Then there was the elderly lady who brought her dog in to be euthanized (that means killed, too) because she couldn't afford the $150 the vet wanted to find out what was wrong with the dog.

The antiquated animal shelter looks and feels like a prison, and many of the dogs act (rightly so) as if they are on death row. At least the Friends of the Long Beach Animal Shelter volunteers would smile at the mention of the soon-to-open animal center near El Dorado Park.

Enough depression. This is about the newest member of the Saltzgaver family. We have been joined by a Shepweiller, a rare breed of dog found only at the Long Beach Animal Shelter. Please don't confuse him with the equally rare Rottherd, which is not nearly as smart. Tiger, who I suspect will eventually tip the scales at more than 125 pounds, would take offense.

This bundle of puppy energy is just two months old, and doesn't have a clue about how close he had come to not seeing three months. He is pure happiness. And watching John (who isn't the most disciplined 11-year-old around) trying to train him to obey brings joy to my heart.

I have to admit, there's one member of the family who isn't too thrilled with the new addition. Hollywood the cat is in a pure funk over it all. But Hollywood has been with me for nine years now, and gone through myriad changes of lifestyle as my life changed. She'll adjust.

This morning, I was out walking a puppy at 5:30 – before my morning tea, no less. I guess I've got some adjusting to do, too. I'm ready. I think the family is too.

After all, we're in puppy love.

LONG BEACH'S DOG beach was one of the first in Southern California. The newspaper had covered it frequently. I had to give it a try, even if it meant a 30-minute drive from home.

It worked out very well.

July 26, 2001

It's a dog's world. At least it was last weekend in Long Beach. And Tiger, our 8-month-old Rottweiler-Shepherd mix, got to get out in it.

This was Tiger's first chance to go partying with other dogs. His previous social engagements have been limited to the chance encounter with another single dog, usually through a fence during walks.

Maria is an extremely protective mother.

But it was my lovely wife who suggested we take advantage of Justin Rudd's brainchild, Haute Dogs on the Beach, to start easing Tiger into the canine social world. I'll have to admit, the image of our 70-pound puppy in the ocean egged me on, as well.

So Sunday afternoon we loaded Tiger into my little sports car for an adventure. The adventure began as soon as I started the car.

You see, my decade-old convertible doesn't have much of a back seat. The one previous time I had allowed Tiger into the car (a trip to the vet), he happily sat in the front seat. Only now Maria was sitting there.

Long story short, after driving through a wrestling match, Tiger spent most of the ride in Maria's lap. Do I need to draw you a picture?

The sight that greeted us at the beach was awesome. There were sailboats, kite boarders, sailboarders, jet skiers and little kid swimmers in the water, all apparently co-existing peacefully. On shore, there were sunbathers, picnickers, volleyballers and little kid sand castle builders, all apparently co-existing peacefully.

And there was a stretch of beach marked off by yellow caution tape. We were early, but it was already filled with dogs of every shape and type. Little yap dogs, carefully groomed pure-breeds, mutts of every size and shape were running, sniffing, swimming and generally being dogs. And all apparently co-existing peacefully – with each other, and with other beach users.

Tiger seemed stunned at first. He didn't seem to know where to turn. So many people to say hi to, so many dogs to sniff!

He greeted a friend of mine, a dog walker/trainer person, by putting his paws on her shoulders. "Hasn't been to obedience school yet, has he?" she asked, eyebrows arching. "He's a dog, not a soldier," I thought, then said aloud, "We're working on it."

We're also working on Tiger coming when he's called, but he's not there yet. And Maria is a very protective mother. So I kept him on his 16-foot leash. That meant I spent most of our time on the sand being pulled up and down the shore, apologizing to people who had been whipsawed by the cord as Tiger followed other dogs around.

The one disappointment was the ocean experience. Our ferocious puppy was afraid of the water. As every baby Long Beach wave approached, Tiger backed away as if it were fire. Even long talks while watching all the retrievers jump through the water couldn't convince him to try for himself.

We went away happy, though, and headed for the dog park in Recreation Park for a little more mellow canine socializing. The dog park has a fence, and Tiger got to wander around without a leash, saying hi to the few dogs who didn't hit the beach.

All in all, Tiger's introduction to dog party town was a success. He'll get to do more, thanks to Rudd and his volunteers, and those dedicated Dog Park folks who have been at this for years.

I thank you and Tiger thanks you. A dog's world isn't a bad place to live.

DOING SOMETHING "FOR someone's own good," especially when you can't explain to that someone what you're doing and why, can be very tough. I found that out – again – with Tiger.

July 3, 2003

I don't think I've ever seen as sad a face as the one I saw this morning.

My dog, Tiger, was going to the vet for some tests. There isn't anything wrong that we're aware of, but it's time for his barrage of adult dog tests as well as a teeth cleaning.

For some reason I'm not really clear about, the vet ordered Tiger to fast before his visit. No food for 12 hours, no water for eight.

I've had to do the same for blood tests, and even a surgery or two. But it's different for a dog.

How do you tell a dog he'll get to eat in a little while? How are you supposed to communicate that you know he's thirsty, but he can't have a drink because it's good for him?

I had the job of making sure Tiger didn't get anything before I went to work. I automatically said, "Get off the couch" as I walked through the living room to the kitchen.

He stopped on his way through and looked at the spot where his food bowl usually is. Then he looked at me. Then back to the empty spot on the floor and back at me again.

Oh, the guilt.

Still half asleep, he wandered into the back yard. He stopped to lap at a small pool of water left behind by the sprinklers; I yelled at him. He's used to it – he knows he's not supposed to drink from that kind of water.

Tiger shrugged his doggie shoulders and did his doggie business. Then he stepped back inside and went to where his water cooler is supposed to be. (Tiger is a Rottweiler-German Shepherd mix, weighs about 85 pounds and easily drinks a gallon of water a day. We literally use a 10-gallon water cooler to make sure he can drink when he wants to.)

No water cooler. This is a first for Tiger. I've let the jug run dry a time or two in the past, but then all he had to do was knock it over and someone would refill it.

"How could you?" his eyes ask. "I've been asleep – I couldn't have done anything wrong. Why are you torturing me this way?"

Somehow, the answer "It's for your own good" doesn't seem adequate. But it's the only answer I have.

After making sure the bathroom door was closed (Tiger learned how to put the toilet lid up a long time ago), I escaped out the front door to go to work.

He whined at me as I closed the door. I didn't see much sense in explaining that Maria (my wife, his mom) would be taking him to the vet soon.

When I get home tonight, Tiger will have forgotten all about this morning. That's the great thing about dogs – they don't hold a grudge. But I'll be nicer than usual anyway.

His face will show surprise at that too. But it will be happy surprise.

I wonder which face I'll remember longer?

DOG STORIES ARE great for some, cat stories are great for others. I liked it best when I could write a dog and cat story. This one is true.

January 15, 2004

How about an animal story? First, let me introduce the characters.

There's Tiger, my 3-year-old German Shepherd-Rottweiler mix. Recent readers have met him before. He's 90 pounds of pure muscle and energy, smart when he wants to be, stubborn constantly, gentle to a fault.

Then there's Hollywood, my 12-year-old tabby cat. I haven't written much about her lately. But she's known as the miracle cat, surviving some extremely experimental (and expensive) surgery when she was around 5 just to prove once again how many lives a cat has.

Hollywood was featured in several early Pinches of Salt, including one that probably sparked more letters than any other. When she was in her cat adolescence – about 3 years old – Hollywood was a hunter extraordinaire. I wrote a column about how she would literally jump off the roof of our house into a tree to catch birds, then proudly bring them to me in the house.

I'm sure you can imagine the response of the bird lovers of the world. I thought for a while that I'd have to put Hollywood in the witness protection program.

Even after her miracle surgery, Hollywood has had a less-than-perfect life. She moved with me to five different homes. Then, in what should have been her golden years, I brought a whole new family into her life.

Just when she thought it couldn't get any worse, we got Tiger. I had to build shelves above the washer and dryer just so the cat could eat in peace.

The dog thinks the cat's a toy; the cat thinks the dog's a pain.

Flash forward to the present. For the last two months, Tiger has been going nuts sniffing all over the house. Nothing would stop him – Tabasco sauce, pepper, nothing.

I called the vet. She suggested that I had a possum or something living under the house. (I had left one vent space open because Hollywood liked to escape there for some peace and quiet.) I dutifully closed all access, spread mothballs and exiled Hollywood back to her shelves above the washer. I washed the baseboards with bleach (and have the stained clothes to prove it).

The dog kept sniffing. Not as badly, but it continued. I broke down and put out mousetraps (secretly, because Maria detests rodents).

Still no change. So this weekend, I discussed the situation with Hollywood. I told her I thought we might have a mouse in the house. I said Tiger wouldn't know what to do with one if he caught it, and she agreed.

I said I knew she was getting awfully old. She just blinked her eyes. Then I said it didn't matter, and gave her a little dish of milk – a treat she almost never gets.

You've guessed the ending by now, haven't you?

When I got up this morning, I found the mouse lying on the dryer. Hollywood had laid it far back so Tiger couldn't get to it. She wanted to make sure I knew who got the job done.

Hollywood purred as I poured her second dish of milk in a week. Then she jumped to her bed on the top shelf and settled in, blinking at me.

I'll let you find your own moral to this story. I'm just glad Hollywood and Tiger are around. They're good people, if you know what I mean.

STORIES ABOUT ANIMALS are right up there with stories about kids when it comes to having an ahh factor. Add a little non-lethal suffering, and you get some sympathy. If you can offer some of the comedy inherent in most animal stories, and you should have a winner.

See what you think.

April 26, 2007

Time for a dog story.

At first glance, Tiger would seem to be invincible. He's about 100 pounds of Rottweiler-German Shepherd mix, with the strength of the Rott and the agility of the Shepherd. One of his favorite pastimes is bouncing off a corner of our 6-foot-tall fence so he can see over that fence at what's in the alley.

At 6 years old, he's in his prime. He loves playing with our littler dog, Sassy, fake grandkid Erik, birds that fly over the yard, etc. He loves life. He carries himself with that unselfconscious confidence seen in top athletes. He's top dog, he knows it, and he doesn't have to prove it to anyone.

Which makes it all the more sad. "It" is Tiger's ultimate nemesis – spring allergies.

Yes, my dog has hay fever, or the equivalent. In past years, it has surfaced as an itching and swollen nose (Tiger was not fond of the Bozo jokes).

This year, the allergy showed itself as itchy, dry skin, particularly on top of his paws. Tiger's idea of scratching is nipping himself (I said he was invincible, not smart). He managed to first create a sore, then let it get infected.

Do you see where this is going? It starts with a visit to the vet (and the first $300 on the credit card) for antibiotics, topical sprays – and a cone.

You've seen them. They are those plastic things that go around a dog's neck, most often so they won't scratch at bobbed ears. The other common use is to stop a dog from biting at irritating sores on their haunches, or in Tiger's case, his paw.

Now I've attempted to describe before how big Tiger is. He's no Great Dane or St. Bernard, but he's a big boy. The only cone that would work on him is the giant economy size.

The thing on his head was the size of a satellite television dish. I swear, when he barked, it echoed.

Apparently, Tiger's senses don't extend to making allowances for foreign objects. To the best of his ability, he carried on as if the space occupied by his head hadn't suddenly increased to four feet in diameter.

Watching him walk through a doorway, suffering whiplash as one side of the cone collided with the doorjamb, was funny in a "Three Stooges" sort of way.

Trying to convince him to back up far enough so a door could be opened was particularly tough – because he couldn't understand why I was laughing so hard.

I've learned to cope with the mess he makes at his water bowl and his food dish, trying to get his face down far enough while pushing against the unyielding plastic torture device. And I've made it a point to stop and scratch behind his ears and around his neck, where he can't reach.

But the most disconcerting experience is when Tiger comes up from behind. His head normally rides about three feet above the ground – waist high. He likes to walk up behind me, sticking his head between my waist and arm, looking for a pat.

Only now, the head never gets there. Instead, I get hit in the butt with a cone. Talk about your ultimate Three Stooges moment.

When I checked this morning, the sore looked nearly healed. Tiger goes back to the vet (did I mention I'm starting a pet health insurance company?) later this week. With luck, we'll be able to start May sans cone.

And Tiger will be, once again, invincible.

20 YEARS OF SALT

THIS IS A bit of a different animal column. This particular animal, fish actually, has been my constant companion for more than two decades. It got me a spot on national radio (an NPR piece) and continues to be a great conversation starter at parties.

Let me introduce you to the grunion.

March 11, 2009

Are you a voyeur?

Come on now, admit it. Everybody gets a little thrill when they see something they weren't meant to see, especially if it involves sex.

Well, it's that time again. Sex is happening on the beach, and the participants don't seem to mind if you watch.

They aren't quite as happy when they are caught and eaten, however.

I'm talking about Southern California's own claim to biological fame, the amazing grunion. I've developed a special relationship with this silvery smelt since coming to Long Beach 17 years ago, and it holds a place in my mind, if not my heart.

The relationship began when I tried to figure out why the paper I was going to work for was called the Grunion Gazette. I'd been saddled with strangely-named papers in the past – the one I cut my teeth on back in Colorado was named the South Fork Tines, as in fork tines, but we managed to make it the best weekly in the state.

I also worked for a daily called the Pueblo Chieftain. Only reference to Indians I ever worked for.

The Grunion has since spawned the Downtown and the Uptown gazettes. But at least for locals, the Grunion remains the brand.

More apologies to the beach denizens who know this story well, but I need to explain what makes the grunion so special (the fish, not the paper).

This fish mates on the beach. That's right, out in the middle of

THE ANIMAL STORIES

the sand where everyone can see it. And think about this – they have to hold their fishy breath the whole time.

The female grunion (insert your own cute name here) rides the high tide onto the beach, then stands on her tail, drilling a hole into the sand. Then the male stud muffin (if you can call a 6-inch sardine a stud or a muffin) wraps himself around the female.

They do their thing, then squirm away from the hole, trying to catch the next wave back out to sea. The whole process usually takes less than 60 seconds (insert your own joke here). A batch of fertilized eggs is left behind, maturing under the sand until the next high tide.

Why anyone would name a newspaper after this slightly risqué fish is beyond me. But I have to admit it is unique, and it only happens on our beaches.

The grunion runs – think salmon runs on a miniature scale – take place during full moons and new moons. That's when the tide is the highest, protecting the eggs. For some reason, they pick the darkest of night high tide instead of the daytime high tide. It might be a survival thing, or maybe they are shyer than I thought.

I've used grunion runs as a cheap date. I've expounded about them on the radio. I've cleverly planted them into Gregorio Luke's infamous Valentine's Day lectures.

But I've never eaten one. Many people do, and catching the grunion legally (bare hands only) can be a challenge. I just can't bring myself to swallow my namesake.

For years, we ran a chart offering days and times of the runs (they last four nights twice a month from March through August). I've been remiss in the last couple of years, though, and feel badly about it. So starting this week, the Grunion Run Chart returns, and it will now appear in the appropriate Downtowns and Uptowns, as well. We'll only run the chart when it is legal to catch them (there's a protected spawning period in April and May). It's a proper homage.

And we'll always remind you to allow the grunion to finish mating before you try to catch them. After all, they'd do it for you.

IN GENERAL, SASSY has been such a good dog she has seldom given me cause to write about her. She was one of those inherited pets – we inherited her after her original owner, our stepson, decided to move back to Colorado and informed us there was no room for the dog.

She's been a great part of the family ever since.

Jan. 27, 2010

The diet thing isn't going so well.

Smaller portions only leave the hunger unsatisfied. If there is food within reach, it's gone. Talk about the See Food diet, this is the Smell Food diet.

Running doesn't seem to do the trick, and there's lots of running. That's usually topped by long walks. Carrying extra weights has gone so far that some are being carried in the mouth.

There's even been the diet pill approach. Those pills might have cut the physical craving or need for food, but they sure didn't stop what seems to be a basic, deeply ingrained drive to eat.

Despite all these valiant efforts, a good five pounds has been gained in the last year. I agree, that doesn't sound like much. But when you start at 65 pounds or so, it makes a difference.

I'm talking about my dog Sassy, of course. What? What about my diet, you say? I resemble that remark. That's an intrusion into my privacy.

Sassy's a dog. She doesn't have any privacy.

No, I don't want to talk about how dogs resemble their masters, and vice versa. Sad brown eyes and a rotund belly describe my younger dog, not me. Honest.

Sassy has gone so far as to eat Tiger's food when he isn't looking. That didn't happen a couple of years ago, but the old boy is getting, well, old, and doesn't seem to care as much as he used to.

Sassy is something called a Bernese Mountain Dog. I had

thought that meant a fat Border Collie until the AKC show came to town. Turns out she's really kind of a scrunched-down version of the purebred, which appears to aspire toward St. Bernard size.

Our vet told us a couple of years ago that she was 20 pounds overweight, and we had to do something about it. Since she weighed about 65 pounds then, that seemed to be a tall order. But everyone said I was supposed to be able to feel her ribs, and that certainly wasn't happening.

We tried for well over a year to get her to lose weight. She still runs around like a puppy, and our surrogate grandson, Erik, keeps her moving constantly when he visits on weekends (that's what 9-year-old boys do).

The expensive diet pills dropped a grand total of one pound after six months. I tried rationing her food, but the aforementioned penchant for finding anything available to eat offset that. Add the sad brown eyes constantly asking why I was "starving" her (now I know where the phrase hangdog expression comes from), and I gave up.

Bottom line, I've decided to let the dog be happy. No, we aren't going overboard and letting her eat anything she wants. But I refuse to torture her anymore, either.

All of which is a very convoluted way to tell Justin Rudd that I sympathize with him as he mourns the passing of Rosie the Bulldog.

Rosie was a symbol for much of what Justin has done in Long Beach over the last decade. The way he pulled the dog in his Radio Flyer wagon seemed to some to be over the top when it came to pampering. I think Justin just gave in to the reality that long walks were too much for Rosie, and he wanted to keep her by his side.

Doctors, veterinarians and good friends all tell us that we are really hurting our children, parents or pets when we indulge them too much. They may be right technically, but I've got to believe there's some emotional giveback here.

Showing your love by indulging just a little makes our dogs happy, if not fit. And a happy dog is one of God's great blessings to man.

Believe it. And have a snack.

THE ANIMAL STORIES

I'VE HAD A number of dogs in my life, and loved almost all of them (I did get rid of one after he literally chewed a hole in the wall). But Tiger has a special place in my heart. He was 100+ pounds of love.

It was hard to say goodbye.

Dec. 15, 2010

Are you ready for Christmas? Is your house ready?

For the most part, we are as ready as can be. There are a few more cards to mail, a few more presents to wrap, but there are lights all over the front yard and decorations all over the house.

But there's one exception. We still haven't put the tree up.

That's certainly not for a lack of holiday spirit – Maria does Christmas in a big way. It's more a matter of logistics – logistics and concern for our big dog, Tiger.

I've written about Tiger before. He's a Rotweiller/Shepherd mix, a big old knothead with a heart of gold and an appearance and bark that stops ne'er-do-wells (and mailmen) in their tracks.

We went to the shelter and picked Tiger out as a puppy right after Christmas 10 years ago. The "we" included Maria's two youngest children, Charlotte and John. I had promised them a dog after they moved here from Colorado.

Today, Charlotte is the mother of one, with a second on the way. John is nearing completion of his first (and likely only) tour in the Marines. Tiger's major interaction with children for the last four years has been surrogate grandchild Erik's weekend visits.

In his prime, Tiger was a 105-pound mass of muscle. He loved to run and hit the corner of the backyard fence, soaring so his head and shoulders cleared the 6-foot barrier and he could see what was happening in the alley.

But, as dog people know, 10 years is a long time in a big dog's life. Tiger's muzzle started turning gray more than a year ago, and he pretty much stopped playing tug-of-war with the younger Sassy, much to her distress, at about the same time.

Then he pretty much stopped eating. That prompted visits to the veterinarian, who did lots of tests, offered some guesses and scratched her head about exactly what was wrong.

She could tell us that the arthritis that plagues most dogs of his breed had moved from his hips into his back. That meant pretty much constant pain any time he changed positions.

The lack of eating was traced to a problem with his liver. Cancer was ruled out, but the vet said only an expensive ultrasound could offer more information, and that might not help.

We opted against the extraordinary care and changed him from dry to canned dog food. That helped for a while, and he still manages to eat most of each serving. Unfortunately, he doesn't seem able to keep much of it down.

Oh, did I mention that he has gone pretty much blind? One eye is clouded over, and he can only see shapes out of the other eye.

Bottom line, we've been reduced to a form of doggie hospice care. His pain medication has gradually increased, and walking around the block is now a major endeavor.

So what does all of this have to do with our lack of a Christmas tree?

Well, our living room is pretty small, and we have to remove one of our two recliners to create enough space for the tree. And Tiger has taken over my recliner as his space.

That's right, I let the dog on the furniture. That happened a long time ago, and I'm certainly not apologizing for it now.

Because of his back, Tiger clearly has a hard time getting comfortable anywhere. One look at him in that chair, and it is a foregone conclusion taking it away would be tantamount to torture.

I've happily relocated temporarily to the couch. I'll stay there as long as Tiger wants to stay in the chair.

But that means the only way we can put a tree up is to move Maria's chair. She has created a habitat around that chair, with her handmade Christmas gift projects, laptop for Skyping with the children, etc. The location – next to the fireplace – also is critical.

But the gift projects are nearly complete, and she feels the same way I do about displacing Tiger, so she's about ready to give up her chair, at least for a short time. The tree likely will be up by the time you read this.

We'll have the Christmas tree for the big day, and if my Christmas wish comes true, Tiger will still be in the chair, too.

HOW DO YOU know when it's time to say that it's time?

Ecclesiastes says, "There is a time for everything, and a season for every activity under everything." The sentiment was turned into a famous song. It also is used frequently when death is near, because everything must die in time.

For Hollywood, it was time.

Sept. 28, 2011

I speak of Hollywood, the miracle cat.

Getting Hollywood was one of the first things we did after moving to Long Beach nearly 20 years ago. We (my wife at the time and I) went to the old animal shelter on Willow Street looking for a pet.

We lived in an apartment, so a dog was out. We looked at the forlorn cats in their little cages. I was almost ready to leave when we came across the little tabby with the club tail.

She clearly was the runt of the litter, and the end of her tail was literally tied in a knot. This truly was a rescue.

We named her Hollywood, thinking we would eventually get a second cat and call it Vine (never happened). She was feisty from the get-go – perhaps a bit more than feisty. Not exactly a lover, this one.

Hollywood got me into trouble often, but never more than the time I wrote a column boasting about her prowess as a hunter. An indoor-outdoor cat, she delighted in bringing me birds and mice. We had to celebrate her successes quietly – wives have a tendency to not appreciate such talents.

Hollywood became a miracle cat after the divorce (which had nothing to do with it). She contracted some mysterious disease that caused her to lose weight rapidly. Since she was less than 10 pounds to begin with, the problem quickly became life threatening.

I admit it. I needed that cat. She was all I had.

I went through a lot of money I didn't have, and ultimately agreed to an experimental surgery.

She survived. We both survived me feeding her through a tube in her throat for a solid month.

Hollywood, the miracle.

Flash forward to today. Hollywood is little more than skin and bones – probably no more than three pounds, if that. Her hips have clearly deteriorated; she looks sort of like a low rider when she walks.

I knew the end was getting near a few months ago, when she stopped fighting the flea treatments. She hated the smell of that stuff, and hid when she could, fought when I caught her. Now she submits quietly.

She walks around the dog now instead of telling her to get out of the way. On more than one occasion, she has failed to make the jump to the top of the trashcan, the first step on the way to her food on top of the dryer (I mentioned we had a dog, right?). That look of humiliation after the fall is more painful than the fall itself.

When Maria took Hollywood to the vet last year, the vet argued that we should put her down (lovely euphemism, that). So Hollywood no longer goes to the vet.

It made sense to me. As far as we can tell, Hollywood is not in pain, and enjoys life like most cats do – mostly by sleeping. Her appetite goes up and down, but she never fails to come and request, make that demand, a treat when there is meat, fish or cheese involved.

She is slowing down slowly. After all, she is more than 19 years old. What's that in cat years?

I have to admit, I was being selfish. I was hoping that she'd pass away peacefully some night in her sleep. I'd bury her and be done with it.

But that hasn't happened. And now Hollywood is losing control of her bladder. She gets up and starts for her cat box, but just can't make it there. She doesn't look upset when the urine comes, just sort of resigned.

I fear that the bowels will be next, and I don't think Hollywood can take that. She remains a proud cat, and that sort of humiliation seems simply unfair.

But she's not in obvious pain, and I can still raise a purr with a scratch in the proper place (behind her right ear). So I still haven't called the vet. But I will, and probably this week.

When I know it's time to say it's time.

THE ANIMAL STORIES

JUST AS THE death of a pet is one of the saddest times in a family, the adoption of a pet is one of the happiest. When you can combine it with a happy holiday such as Christmas, well, it doesn't get much better than that.

Dec. 22, 2011

Call me sentimental.

I'd like to think I'm not – sentimental, that is – but every once in a while, my actions betray me.

Which, in a roundabout way, is the reason why there's an exuberant canine with a whip for a tail bounding around my house even as we speak. I let my sentiments get the upper hand over my rational curmudgeonliness.

It starts, as most good Christmas stories do, with a bit of a tragedy.

As Christmas 2010 approached, my good big dog Tiger's health was failing rapidly. The Rottweiler-Shepherd mix was more than 10 years old, and had been losing weight for a while. Then he started showing signs of confusion and distress.

It was a sad day less than a week before Christmas 2010 (Dec. 20, if memory serves), when we said goodbye to Tiger. We mourned the loss of a family member.

Flash forward to September 2011. Maria disappeared for a half hour or so at the Belmont Shore Car Show, and later confessed to going to the German Shepherd Rescue booth.

I managed to dodge the talk of another dog primarily by focusing on Sassy, our sort-of Bernese Mountain Dog. She's a good dog, but needy. She clearly needed all our attention.

Then, right after Thanksgiving, Hollywood the Miracle Cat finally gave up the ghost. She was 19 years old and had used up about 18 of her nine lives. Still, it was hard to say goodbye.

For the last few weeks, Maria has been just a touch mopey. Not so much that it was painful, but enough that it was clear things weren't just right as the holiday season picked up steam.

I might have been able to stand that, but Sassy started moping around, too. She had never played with Hollywood (I think she was scared of the five-pound cat), so I was at a bit of a loss about the cause. She clearly was lonely, though.

So I started looking around. I made a call to John Keisler, the guru of the Long Beach Animal Shelter who has recently added the burden of business manager of Parks, Recreation and Marine to his plate. I'm still a Parks and Rec commissioner, so he took my call, and promised to keep a lookout for a shepherd or Rott coming through the P.D. Pitchford Animal Village.

Then last week I had a few minutes and decided to check the Seal Beach Animal Shelter website. Seal Beach also advertises with us, and I figured it couldn't hurt to just browse.

Boy, was I wrong.

Seal Beach is a relatively small shelter. It's a no-kill facility, so their turnover isn't all that great. When I checked the website, they had about 15 dogs in their "available to adopt" queue.

I skipped past the Chihuahuas and the fox terrier. I ignored the Dachshund and stopped only briefly at the Cocker, even though I had had one as a boy. (In one of her wistful imaginings, Maria had made it clear Cockers weren't big enough.)

I was ready to get back to work when I saw the last entry. It was a dog named – you guessed it – Tiger. He was listed as a shepherd-lab mix. The original owners apparently named him Tiger because there is a hint of stripes in his brindle coat.

The dog had been born – you guessed it again – in December 2010. He had been at the animal shelter for about six months, given up mainly because the original owners couldn't keep both the puppies and the mom.

Maria and I visited Friday afternoon. I have seldom met a dog with a more loving, willing-to-please temperment. They said he was a year old, but he still acted like a puppy – something pretty incredible when you realize he'd spent half of his life in a 5' by 15' kennel. That says all sorts of good things about how SBAC cares for its charges.

Long story short, we came back the next day with Sassy for a meet-and-greet, and ended up taking Tiger – now officially Tiger Too – home with us.

Christmas cheer has been reestablished in the Saltzgaver home. Tiger loves to play, sleeps sprawled all over the sofa just like Tiger One did, and does just enough bad stuff to remind us he's a pup.

I'm smiling. And I'm not too terribly sorry that I'm just a touch sentimental.

Merry Christmas to all.

Part TWO
Stories In The News

STORIES IN THE NEWS

I WAS GREETED to my new job as executive editor at Gazette Newspapers with the biggest story of the decade in Southern California. A video of the beating of Rodney King had been seen around the world, and countless times here.

So when a Simi Valley jury found the officers involved innocent on all counts, Los Angeles exploded. It spread quickly to Long Beach. In a sign of the times, the biggest complaint we got about our coverage was the fact that I had the temerity to call them "race riots" in our lead headline.

The politically correct phrase was "civil unrest." Really.

May 7, 1992

How do you talk about a return to normalcy in the face of what we've experienced in the last week?

If the words flowing about the Rodney King verdict and its violent aftermath were worth a penny apiece, there would be no more poverty in the world. But the fact is, it's a situation that cannot be ignored.

This is my third column for this paper, and already I have been forced by circumstance to break my vow to keep this space light. But it seems the height of insensitivity to write about my weekend on the beach, or culture shock in the Southland.

Much of the verbiage in newspapers, on radio and television, talk about healing, joining together. Important words, to be sure.

But I get a sense of longing underneath it all. A longing to return to something resembling a normal life.

That doesn't have to mean – shouldn't mean – ignoring the underlying causes of last week's violence. It would be foolish to think that racial tension or poverty will just fade away if we don't think about them.

Perhaps a little bit of my '60s idealism remains, because I'd like to think that dealing with those issues is part of normal life. A life without problems wouldn't be much of a normal life, either.

I guess my major concern is trying to deal with the complex issues of race and poverty in the caldron of finger-pointing that already has begun.

There is no doubt people responsible for the violence – from government officials who ignored the situation to the looters who carted off storefuls of merchandise – should be held to account. But frankly it is less than reassuring to hear President Bush talk of bringing the federal justice system to bear – to redress what the public perceives as an injustice – in a knee-jerk reaction to placate the Afro-American community.

What I'm trying to get to is that the underlying causes of the violence in Long Beach, Los Angeles and other parts of the country are not going to be solved through impassioned speeches or virulent accusations. If we are going to make any real progress in making this world a better place to live. It is only going to be done in a constructive, not a destructive, environment.

People will return to the beaches this weekend. People will return to the restaurants and stores. They will try to get on with their lives, but the issues of race and poverty remain.

And at least for me, that is a start to a return to what should be normalcy.

STORIES IN THE NEWS

JUST A FEW months after I arrived in Long Beach, and less than a year after moving from Colorado to California, the earth flexed its muscles in what came to be known as the Northridge Earthquake. The quake was strong enough to provide some serious shaking in Long Beach, but essentially no damage.

Oblivious of the damage done elsewhere, I treated it lightly.

July 7, 1992

Had enough earthquake stories yet? I hope not, because I've got one more.

Let me back into this. Oldest daughter, Melanie, flew back to Colorado on Sunday. I had promised her for days that her last weekend would be a particularly California one.

We hit the Shore for dinner Saturday night, then headed out for a night of miniature golf. Melanie and I sat and watched the fancy cars driving up and down Second Street, so I guess that was sort of California.

But outside of an hour or so on the freeway to the golf place and back, I didn't think we had captured the essence of Southern California the way I had hoped. It wasn't a failure of an evening at all — just not quite what I had in mind.

Mother Nature decided to step in. I was awakened at 5 a.m. by the waves of the waterbed. The thing started serious swells before I figured out what was going on.

Younger daughter Michelle, camping out on the floor in the living room that night, rode out the temblor like an amusement park ride. Son Derek heard a neighbor's wind chimes and thought it was raining (he doesn't wake up any too quickly).

Then we heard the voice from the other room - "Mom? Mom!"

Maybe Melanie was the only one old enough to realize she was supposed to be scared of earthquakes, I thought. But once the shaking stopped, even she seemed happy to have gone through the experience.

When the second quake hit at 8 that morning, she was almost ecstatic. Now she had something really California to regale her Colorado friends with. She had been in not one, but two honest-to-gosh earthquakes.

The kids' response, as well as listening to literally terrified people on a radio call-in show, set me to wondering about my own reaction. Frankly, I thought it was a kick.

Don't get me wrong. I'm well aware of the potential danger of earthquakes. And I'll admit to some serious fear over the fact that there's literally no place to hide from one.

But are my wife and I contemplating leaving because of the threat of the "Big One?" 'Fraid not.

Part of it, I suppose, is a fatalistic streak in my philosophy. When it's my time, it will be my time no matter how it comes.

There have been several incidents in my life where I probably should have shuffled off this mortal coil. And I still ride a motorcycle every day – a practice my boss assures me will make any pension plan unnecessary.

Perhaps a bigger part of my seeming unconcern is the realization that no matter where you live, you face the potential for a killer catastrophe.

I've personally been caught in a blizzard on the plains of Colorado, waiting two hours for a snowplow rescue. I've helped dig people out of avalanches in the mountains. I've stood on the roof of an office building watching tornadoes in the distance, and I've toured areas where the twisters did their damage. I've been with the firefighters during a forest fire.

I haven't witnessed a hurricane, except through the wonders of television. But I have covered floods, and droughts.

I know. None of that alleviates the danger – the terror – of an earthquake. And I certainly don't want to sound like I'm ignoring all the work gone in to making buildings earthquake-proof, nor am I belittling those who stock up with earthquake kits.

But I must admit I managed to go back to sleep Sunday morning after the first quake. And at least at last reality check, I don't think I'll lose any sleep waiting for the next one.

A BIT OF background here – I was an English major. That should be enough to explain this take on education but at the time I also was chair of the board for the Public Corporation for the Arts, Long Beach's arts council. The point of view becomes clear quickly here.

Jan. 18, 2001

It appears that the education pendulum finally is beginning to swing back to an understanding of the importance of the arts and humanities. Last week, the state Department of Education quietly released new standards that "will guide school districts in developing comprehensive arts education programs at all grade levels." It's no surprise that in today's test-happy world that the pendulum swing back to the arts has to be couched in "standards," but it's a start (even if the standards are recommendations, not requirements).

From my perspective, education in America began its most recent decline in the 1970s, when the "Back to Basics" movement gained favor. The increasingly high-tech work world scared the bejeesus out of educators, who were afraid that teaching anything not connected to math and science was a waste of time.

Add the education funding slashing of the late 1980s and 1990s, and music and art classes all but disappeared in the schools. No more elementary school choir or band, and finger painting from kindergarteners was about the only art left to put on school walls.

I'm all in favor of the three "Rs," (Reading, wRiting and 'Rithmetic), and when I'm pushed, I'll say that reading is the number one thing youngsters must learn. But it appears to me that the lack of arts programs in the schools for the last few decades has spawned a generation who think on the surface – if they think at all.

Of course, it wasn't that concern for education of the soul that caused the pendulum to begin moving. It took studies that showed students with a good arts background scored higher on standardized tests (84 points higher on the SAT) and were more likely to graduate from high school.

I contend that the reason for those facts is that arts education teaches children how to think – how to use their whole brain. The fact that it touches a portion of human beings not necessarily concerned with the bottom line is critical. Delaine Eastin, the state Superintendent of Public Instruction, may have said it best:

"The standards come at a time when there is increased recognition by educators, researchers and the public that, through a visual and performing arts program. our students will learn to participate in and contribute to society in intelligent and sensitive ways."

As usual, the education system in Long Beach is in the forefront of this movement. Thanks in large part to the outreach efforts of the Long Beach Symphony and other arts groups, the arts retained a tenuous foothold in the schools. Then a couple of years ago, Superintendent Carl Cohn was able to find the money to hire an arts education coordinator.

Still using the resources of the arts community at large, Long Beach schools began to create more art programs. The school district partnered last year with the Public Corporation for the Arts to create the first in-school "Smithsonian" museums, and has stepped up this year to become a true partner in Smithsonian Week in Long Beach. Cohn was instrumental in setting up the Music & Art for the Millennium project with the symphony and the Long Beach Museum of Art (I'm going to a concert today at Lowell Elementary School to see it first-hand).

More books, smaller classes, better facilities – all are great needs in our schools today. A chance to touch our children's souls is just as great a need. Let's all push the pendulum a little harder.

SCHOOL SHOOTINGS BECAME far too common as we entered the 21st Century. The shooting in San Diego hit home in more ways than one.

March 8, 2001

It's a tragedy. It's a travesty. It's obscene. It's unfathomable. Once again, a young boy has decided enough is enough, and sought revenge on those who had picked on him. Deadly revenge. With a gun.

Two students dead, 13 more injured. Reportedly all because they had the mean-spirited but regrettably common youthful habit of calling a 15-year-old peer hurtful names.

At least that's what the "experts" blame the bloody tragedy on. Sorry, but I don't buy it. Charles Andrew Williams was and is responsible for his own actions.

But that doesn't lessen the tragedy or the burning desire to do something – anything – to make this insanity stop.

Many of the news reports are comparing this incident in east San Diego with the Columbine High School shootings in Colorado two years ago. I wrote a column about that shooting, citing my Colorado connections as the reason for my personal concern.

This time around, I have a much stronger cause for concern. Their names are Charlotte and John. They go to school – a place that once was a safe refuge for our children. These days, despite the relative rarity of true violence, sending your kids to school feels more than a little scary.

These days, a kid saying he's going to shoot up the campus must be "kidding" or blowing off steam. Williams told family and friends what he was going to do, then said he was kidding. So no one did anything.

And a tragedy ensued.

These days, high school campuses are fenced and police officers are stationed outside or roam the halls. Searches for weapons are routine. Some schools have already installed airport-style met-al detectors, and it wouldn't surprise me to see X-ray machines for backpacks before the year is out.

That's sad. Probably necessary, but sad.

These days, getting a gun is as easy as getting a Walkman. How on God's green earth did a 15-year-old have access to a pistol and enough ammunition to pull the trigger "at least 30 times?"

The ubiquitous National Rifle Association issued a press release hours after the shooting calling for the boy to be tried as an adult and face the death penalty "to send a message." Thanks, Charlton, but it seems like the message has been sent.

These days, the entertainment world touts guns as the great equalizer. Movies depict the bloodied, battered good guy blowing away the enemy. The vast majority of video games, at least those played by teen-aged boys, are based on killing the bad guy.

So who can blame the poor picked-on freshman for taking fantasy and making it reality, right? I don't think so.

These days, California is ranked dead last in the number of high school counselors per student (state Supervisor of Public Instruction Delaine Eastin's words, not mine). If the boy had just gone to a counselor instead of the gun cabinet, though …

As a society, we have to do what we can on all those fronts to make our children safer. As much as I want to say that parents should take responsibility for teaching their own the difference between right and wrong — and as much as I believe that — these days it appears impossible to expect all parents to do that.

We protect ourselves as best we can, including doing everything possible to improve the environment so violence is less of an option. But ultimately, we have to admit that there is evil in this world, and evil things happen.

I urge my children and yours to take responsibility for their own actions, and I'll do what I can to make sure you make the right choices. And I'll pray to God for your safety.

Please stop. Please think. Please leave the damned guns alone.

Stop the tragedy.

AFTER NATURAL GAS price spikes in the winter, there was an outcry for "justice" in the form of rebates of discounts. The concept of the city being forced to pass on the high cost it had to pay for the gas seemed lost on many. At least that's how I saw it.

May 3, 2001

We've met the enemy, and they is us. I think that's from an old Pogo comic strip, but I don't know if I've got the words just right, so I won't call it a quote. Still, it certainly seems true these days in Long Beach.

Let me phrase it another way. We've met the government, and they is us. I wish more people would realize that when they lobby for tax rebates, subsidized electricity and the like.

Our beloved City Hall critics continue to cry for not just lower natural gas bills but for some sort of payback of high bills last winter. And while they're at it, they'd like to totally eliminate the tax on gas, electricity and the like.

I'd like lower bills, too. Trust me, with two kids in the house, I'm feeling the pinch (pun intended).

But I know that if I expect the city to bail me out, something has to give elsewhere. That's what seems to be lost on the "activists."

Let me phrase it another way. There's no such thing as a free lunch.

Doesn't it seem rational that if the city is forced to find millions of dollars to satisfy those braying for utility bill relief that there would be less money to provide city services? Money, like natural gas, is a limited commodity, and if you put it one place you have to take it away from another place.

Unless, of course, you think city officials are just sandbagging and actually have all the money they need to provide for your every whim and still cut your tax bill. That seems to be the attitude of the more radical critics. In fact, some would have you believe the nefarious city leaders are guilty of malfeasance, fraud and more.

Ironically, city management has fed that attitude by doing some extremely creative work to get things done when money was tight. The emergency communications center finally on the horizon is a prime example – after being thwarted in efforts to come up with "easy" ways to pay for the center, the then-city manager, James Hankla, "found" the money elsewhere (he took a new mortgage on City Hall). That led to plenty of "I told you they had it" comments.

The latest brouhaha is over the "discovery" that the city's gas department has made a profit in recent years. "We should get our gas at cost!" the outraged activists cry. "How could you profit on the back of the citizens? It's fraud, I say."

Bull. That "profit" went directly into the general fund to pay for city services – you know, police officers, firefighters, street repairs, that kind of stuff. If the money doesn't come from selling natural gas, there are two choices. Raise taxes (fat chance in this day and age) or cut services.

"Scare tactics," the activists moan. "They've got the money. They always have the money. Cut our bills, cut our taxes. And we'll fire you if you don't keep (and improve) our services."

Saying the "citizens" shouldn't pay as much as they pay is easy, and popular. Saying how the services those same citizens expect should be paid for is harder. That's why I'm not too surprised I haven't heard any of those types of suggestions from our activist friends.

Sounds to me like they're looking for a free lunch.

UNDOUBTEDLY, VIRTUALLY EVERY columnist in the country addressed the 9-11 attacks. Portions of my piece were quoted in industry publications about how journalists respond to these disasters.

September 13, 2001

   I'm numb. I think maybe the whole nation is numb. I'm writing this on Tuesday morning, with CNN on the television next to me. It seems as if there's been a flash of a new attack every 15 minutes since I got up this morning.
   I wasn't born when the Japanese bombed Pearl Harbor. But I think now I might know how my parents and grandparents felt.
   Scared. Uncertain. Helpless. And mad.
   There doesn't seem to be much reason for me to go over the details of the attacks here – if you haven't heard them all by now, you're deliberately avoiding it. Multiple hijackings, jets crashing into buildings, thousands of lives lost, an entire nation shut down – all apparently the act of terrorists.
   Fingers pointing swung almost immediately to Afghanistan and Osama bin Laden, the "chief terrorist" in the world today. But why?
   There is speculation that the attackers have ties to the Palestinians. The Camp David accords, where the current separation of Israel between Arabs and Jews was first hammered out, were reached around this time in 1978.
   At least this morning, the motivation is secondary. We are under attack, and the fear and uncertainty dominates.
   When I got to the office this morning, one of the women who work here asked me if we were safe. I hated my answer – "I don't know."
   The kids are at school – that's got to be as safe a place as any. Maria's working at home – again, as safe a place as any. We're pushing ahead here, trying to put out our community newspaper.

I guess that's what you do in the face of this type of epic tragedy – keep on keeping on. I just wish I could do more.

Long Beach has responded to the threat (see story, Page 1A) properly. But if this morning has taught us anything, no preparation or response is enough to stop insane, irrational attacks.

I'm praying that I don't have to go out and actually cover any tragedy here today or tomorrow. I've done it more than once in my career (plane crashes, fires, riots), and it's one of the toughest things about this job. They also weren't anything near this scale.

But if it happens, I, we, will be there. It's our job, and it's an important one. Why? Because the only way to ease the uncertainty is to have someone able to say what's going on, and that someone is the media.

What comes next? I hate my answer to this one too – "I don't know."

America will retaliate. The question is, how and against whom? Do we attack a country? Is this the opening salvo in World War III? That seems doubtful.

But it will change our lives. Prepare for even more security here, particularly if you fly. Remember what the airports were like after the rash of hijackings in the 1970s? It will be that times 10.

Tensions will run high, both at home and around the world. We're living in a hair-trigger world again, folks, and it's not going to be fun.

Keep on keeping on. And pray. We're all going to need it.

20 YEARS OF SALT

LIKE EVERYONE ELSE, I was consumed with 9-11 and our many and varied responses. I tried not to write about it too often, but succumbed here.

Nov. 1, 2001

"Calling Dr. Bombay, calling Dr. Bombay. Emergency. Come right away!"

For you youngsters, and those not subjected to 1960s sitcoms growing up, that line comes from the TV show "Bewitched." Elizabeth Montgomery, playing Samantha, the savvy witch with the ditzy husband, uttered it any time magical doctoring was required. (Why she married the fool and didn't wait for me, I still don't know. But that's another story.)

I suppose this shows the power of hypnosis inherent in the boob tube, but that line has become sort of a mantra for me when things are so messed up that there seems to be no manmade solution. When Dr. Bombay did come, he invariably made things worse before they got better. But it was a sure bet Samantha would be calling him again in the next few episodes.

I think many of our leaders are calling Dr. Bombay these days. No one has a real clue how to stop individuals bent on evil with a plethora of ways to do their dirty deeds. Hijacking airplanes and mailing anthrax just happen to be the first two ideas they pulled out of the hat.

I hate to sound pessimistic here, but frankly, that's how I feel. Here's why.

For the last 45 days, the whole country has been on red alert. The mobilization of the federal government has been nothing short of incredible. The resources thrown into the war against terrorism have been nothing short of incredible too.

Something like 7,000 FBI agents were assigned to the terrorism case. I didn't even know there were that many agents in the whole bureau. A brand-new Cabinet-level department was formed for "home defense." A bill has been passed giving surveillance powers to police and police-type agencies the likes of which have never before been seen in this country. It appears likely now that federal employees will soon scrutinize every piece of luggage in every airport.

And there's the little matter of military action in Afghanistan.

Although it seldom is seen in the papers these days, the recovery and cleanup at the World Trade Center towers plods on, with bodies and body parts recovered every day. Four people have died so far from anthrax exposure. That's a far cry from the 6,000 or so who died Sept. 11, but just as scary.

The Senate office building has closed, as have a number of post offices and even the U.S. Supreme Court, because of anthrax scares. Postal workers don't get hazardous duty pay yet, but they probably should. People are working hard, trying hard to eliminate the danger.

So Monday, Attorney General John Ashcroft issues a "terror alert." He said a terrorist attack is likely in the next week. He also said the government doesn't know where, when or how it will happen. But the American people "need to know, so they can be vigilant

I sure don't have any answers about how to deal with this very real threat that surrounds us like smoke. I have no doubt that those in charge are more than competent.

But I really want to say, "Calling Dr. Bombay, calling Dr. Bombay. Emergency. Come right away!"

YET ANOTHER 9-11 terrorist attack-related issue. As the first Christmas after the attacks approached, charities were very worried about declining donations.

Nov. 29, 2001

I'm here to put your mind at ease. You don't have to worry about what to get me for Christmas anymore.

I know that burning question – What does Harry need? – has been causing sleepless nights. Well, let the Sandman come. Here's the answer.

Make a donation to your favorite charity.

It's hard to believe, but I'm eschewing all those wonderful donations to the Saltzgaver Debt Relief Fund in favor of the plethora of good causes found in Long Beach. Besides, my application for a 501(c)(3) nonprofit status is still pending. They can't seem to find a category for the amount of red ink I'm spilling.

More important, our folks who do all the good work in fair Long Beach are hurting in a big way. Virtually every organization that counts on the generosity of donors has become a secondary victim of the terrorists who perpetrated the Sept. 11 disasters.

Don't get me wrong. The incredible outpouring of support for the victims at and around the World Trade Center has been nothing short of phenomenal. The selfless giving gives hope that there might be something good about us humans after all.

But (and there's always a but, isn't there?) a fair share of that money has been siphoned away from the many groups that make living in Long Beach a little better. The loss has been felt in everything from direct giving to attendance at fundraisers. I even got an unbelievable deal at the Chamber of Commerce golf tournament silent auction, mainly because no one else was bidding.

I'm talking to all you CEOs out there, too. I know you read this column, even if you do hide it when someone comes into the room.

Corporate sponsorship has become the mainstay of many nonprofits, from those working with the homeless to the many arts organizations that help make life worth living. Many corporations put major bucks into the New York City relief effort, and that is commendable. Now it is time to get back to giving to those who make our American lives worth fighting for.

Your options are virtually endless. Whether you drop a coin in that Salvation Army kettle or write a big check to the Volunteers of America, you will be making a difference. You'll feel good about it, too.

If you want something in return for your generosity, and that warm fuzzy feeling isn't enough, you could always attend one of the many theatrical or musical programs put on during the holiday season. (Why not match that ticket price as a donation while you're at it?) Or you could patronize one of the nonprofit groups' gift boutiques sprouting up this month to do your holiday shopping.

As I said, the options go on and on

The Bible says to give until it hurts, and Jesus tried to convince the rich man to give away all of his possessions. I wouldn't presume to offer the same admonition, since I can't live up to it myself. But I will ask that you give what you can, every time you can.

It really does make a difference. It makes life a little brighter for someone less fortunate than you, and it allows people to create some of that soul food that enriches our own lives.

To receive a gift is fun. To give a gift is divine. I hope you have the chance to experience a bit of both this holiday season.

That would be a great gift for me.

MILESTONE COLUMNS AFTER the 9-11 terrorist attacks quickly became a must. Here's how it felt six months after the fact.

March 14, 2002

Six months and the world has changed. As beacons of light reached for the stars in New York City as a memorial to those who died in the Twin Towers on Sept. 11, 2001, American soldiers were fighting in Afghanistan. As a small brass plaque was placed in front of the Pentagon to remember the 189 who died there on Sept. 11, the generals inside mused on when and where it might be appropriate to use nuclear weapons.

In many ways, our lives have returned to "normal" in the wake of Sept. 11, just as President Bush wanted. Shaq and the Lakers are waking up in time for the playoffs, the Dodgers are sure they've got the winning combination down in Vero Beach, the movie industry is ready to give out its naked (but androgynous) gold statues while patting each other on the back.

Most of us go to work in the morning, and go home to our families in the evening. The economy is humming along again, belying the fear that Bin Laden had struck a mortal blow. City politicos talk of sidewalks and alleys (and cops, to be sure) as they vie for a term in office.

So why does the atmosphere today remind me so much of that era when I was routinely duck-and-covering under my school desk? Why am I craving a home with an honest-to-gosh basement, complete with foot-thick concrete walls and a way to seal the entrance from the fallout?

I was just a kid, literally, in the late 1950s and early '60s, when it seemed certain that the man who banged his shoe (Nikita Khrushchev, youngsters) was determined to blow up the world. The class films of Hiroshima were fresh enough to have us ducking under those desks with a will.

But youthful optimism convinced me that even adults wouldn't be stupid enough to willfully destroy us. In fact, I'm fairly certain that my constant wishes on a star (thanks, Jiminy Cricket) were a main factor in our survival in that Cold War.

Sadly, I've grown up.

Some of my newfound dread undoubtedly comes from the release of a report wherein our country's leaders map out scenarios to use nuclear weapons. That map goes further than eliminating the Red Menace, too. We're talking up to seven countries here, and scales ranging from retaliatory Doomsday strikes to surgical "bunker-busting" with nuclear warheads.

I'm old enough to know our military leaders have been creating nuclear weapon strategies since before the Manhattan Project. I'm world-weary enough to know that that's their job, and that having a plan isn't the same as implementing it.

But my Cold War memory tells me that once one nuclear weapon is used, another is sure to follow. That's when all Hell — again, literally — breaks loose.

I'm not quite ready to build my bomb shelter, though. I guess there's still a little Jiminy Cricket left somewhere deep in my psyche. There's just enough optimism left to hope and pray that rational adults aren't stupid enough to willfully cause our destruction - despite growing evidence to the contrary.

I'll keep on with my life, worrying more about my family and my job than the fate of the world. It's the only thing I can do. But in the back of my mind, one fact rises large and refuses to be ignored.

The world has changed.

I'VE ALWAYS BEEN big on taking responsibility. But it should be people taking responsibility, not animals. When a rash of dog attacks hit the news, I decided to hit back.

March 28, 2002

Everyone who owns a dog, raise your hand. Everyone who owns a big dog, raise both your hands.

Everyone who can't control their big dog, raise both hands and one foot.

For those of you now tottering on one leg, I have a bit of unsolicited advice. Get rid of your dog.

Oh, everyone who owns a Presa Canario, raise both hands and both legs. You've just fallen on your rear end, and you can't get up.

I'm a dog lover. I had dogs when I was a small boy, a large boy, a college boy and a young married boy. I, or rather my family and I, have a dog now. A big dog.

The latest dog mauling, where a Canary Islands fighting dog killed a woman while the dog allegedly was in the control of his owner, has given me cause for pause. Perhaps even worse were the stories that dog breeders couldn't find enough Presa Canarios to fulfill the demand from those who were panting to have the biggest, baddest thing around.

Just like people, there are good dogs and bad dogs. And just like people, most of their behavior is a product of the environment in which they are raised. It's not the breed, it's the individual.

But convince the public of that.

When I was growing up, the macho dog title belonged to the Doberman Pinscher. I think it had something to do with a James Bond movie. At any rate, I was terrified of the things.

That is, I was until I met a nice guy who had raised a Doberman. The dog was, pardon the pun, a pussycat.

In the 1990s, pit bulls were the thing. They aren't all that big – 50 or 60 pounds – but tenacious was an understatement when describing them. Being attacked by a pack was second only to falling into a pool of piranha when it came to describing terror.

When we went to the pound about 13 months ago to pick out a dog, John and Charlotte found a truly cute puppy. But there was no adoption number on the cage, so I sought out a volunteer to see how we could go about getting the pup.

"We can't let that one go out for adoption," the volunteer said. "It's part pit bull."

Talk about being damned by the company you keep.

I wasn't looking for a big dog or a guard dog when we chose Tiger. We adopted him because he loved the kids, not because he was half German Shepherd and half Rottweiler. But he started causing people to cross the street when we went on walks before he was six months old.

Tiger weighs about 90 pounds now, and is stronger than most men twice that size. He's most comfortable carrying around a dinosaur-sized bone – or patiently playing with his bud, 15-month-old Eric.

Tiger and I walk around our neighborhood a lot. Our area is blessed with lots conducive to big back yards, and you don't really fit in unless you keep a dog. Most of my neighbors have two.

And most of them are – the barking symphony as we take the nightly walk sounds like an all-bass choir. There are German Shepherds, a gorgeous full-blooded Rottweiler and even some pit bulls living within a block of me.

But they all live in big back yards, not apartments like the now-executed Bane did in San Francisco before he became a killer. In my experience, they're all well behaved, with a lot of bark and very little bite.

I'll always be careful around strange dogs, and teach my children to do the same. I'll also always cringe every time I see someone trying to create a weapon out of a dog.

But I know dogs are individuals, just like people. It's the individual, not the race, that matters.

So, dog owners, raise your children, I mean dogs, well. That way, you can keep both feet on the ground.

STEVE HORN SERVED 10 years in Congress as a moderate Republican representing Long Beach. That came after a career in higher education, including a stint as president of California State University, Long Beach. His success can be measured by the fact the Democrats redistricted his district out of existence.

Dec. 5, 2002

So when is the ticker tape parade? Where's the key to the city? A Long Beach hero is returning home. But the homecoming has been way too quiet, at least so far.

Of course, Steve Horn would probably disagree. Quiet is his style. Quietly effective, that is.

For the last decade, Steve Horn has represented Long Beach in the U.S. Congress. A former president of California State University, Long Beach, Horn never lost an election. He first ran when the 38th Congressional District was formed after the 1990 census, and retired when it was gerrymandered out of existence after the 2000 census.

For 10 years, we had a congressman we could call our own. Now we're represented by a Huntington Beach surfer and a Carson activist. It is our loss.

Here are just a few things that happened while Mr. Horn was in Washington, D.C.

A federally-mandated flood control project on the Los Angeles River was actually paid for by the federal government and completed early, saving Long Beach residents tons of money by eliminating a federally-mandated flood insurance requirement.

The C-17 military cargo plane program was not only saved, but expanded. It could be argued that Horn single-handedly kept Boeing in Long Beach.

Federal money came down the track in a timely manner for the Alameda Corridor. While you might not know it driving the 710, the corridor is a life extender, and lifesaver, for the movement of cargo from the Port of Long Beach.

The predicted collapse of the federal government computer network as we entered the new millennium didn't happen. You may not believe it now, but Horn's work to avert the Y2K meltdown may in the long run be his crowning achievement.

But all that is only the accomplishment side of Steve Horn. The true value of this Long Beach treasure is in the man himself.

I've been fortunate to know Steve, as well as his super wife Nini and great son Steve Jr., pretty much since the day I came to Long Beach. I think you'll know what I mean when I say that I thought at first they were too good to be true - being that nice had to be an act. But it's no act; it's just the way they are.

Horn's biggest accomplishment in his 10 years in Washington, at least to me, is leaving as the same man who went there in the first place. Steve Horn is a genuinely nice man. The fact he also is intelligent, perceptive and effective is gravy.

Maybe there is some poetic justice in Long Beach losing its own Congressional seat. After all, I can't imagine a politician active today who could fill Horn's shoes, at least as a person. Now no one has to try.

It's time for a ticker tape parade, for a presentation of the key to the city. Long Beach has a hero who should be honored. Until then, there's only one thing to say.

Thank you, Steve.

STORIES IN THE NEWS

THE WEEKS BEFORE Desert Storm were filled with both tension and a sense of inevitability. This was my attempt to capture that feeling.

March 6, 2003

When I was a kid, I had this recurring dream.

I was in a totally silent space, rolling up a huge ball of twine. Dick Tracy (honest) was keeping guard, gun drawn. I was scared to death, because I knew if I made the slightest noise, the whole world would come crashing down.

And I knew I would make a noise.

There's no doubt all the dream interpreters out there will find great meaning in that. I kind of hope they will keep their interpretations to themselves.

I recount it now because it evoked the same feelings I get when I watch our president march toward war.

"There's nothing Saddam can do now to stop war." I heard that quote yesterday on National Public Radio. I'm not sure if it came from President Bush, Colin Powell or one of the myriad press pundits whose sole purpose in life these days is explaining why the president thinks the way he does.

But no matter the source, the statement pretty much sums up the atmosphere in our country right now. It seems war is inevitable. Every time someone – Hussein, the Turks, the United Nations – does something that would seem to set back the chances of war, Bush says or does something to show just how adamant he is about pushing forward.

Early this week, our government cut a deal with the Turkish government to pay them $15 billion in one form or another to allow us to base troops there. That's $15,000,000,000. In a time of budgetary recession. To mount an invasion to protect, at least partially, the country we're paying.

And the Turkish parliament said no. What's up with that?

Of course, Bush said he was reluctant to take no for an answer. He might have even convinced them to change their minds (or made them an offer they couldn't refuse) by the time this column reaches you.

But Bush won't wait. Like Chinese water torture, the steps toward war keep wearing away.

While diplomats ranted and raved at Turkey, the USS Nimitz and its battle group steamed away from San Diego this week. It will take a month for the aircraft carrier and its destroyers (one of the most descriptive names in all military-dom) to reach position. But no one's saying whether the Nimitz is on its way to play a USS Missouri-like role as a post-war enforcer or whether the war will wait until the carrier's planes can reach Iraq.

I abhor the thought of war. I abhor it almost as much as I abhor the thought of what Saddam Hussein has done or could do.

But I have to admit, I think I abhor this state of constant tension even more. It's like tightening a bowstring to the very edge of its breaking point, then setting the bow down and walking away.

Sooner or later, something is going to snap.

Someone is going to make a noise. And all the Dick Tracys in the world can't keep it from happening.

That's no dream. It's a nightmare.

Will someone please wake me up?

STORIES IN THE NEWS

THE RIGHT TO die has been a hotly debated topic ever since the technology has become available to keep people alive beyond their natural time of death. The Terria Schiavo episode dominated news for a good two months, and touched me personally.

March 24, 2005

My favorite line in one of my all-time favorite movies, "Little Big Man," is "Today is a good day to die."

The phrase, a Native American aphorism uttered by Chief Dan George in the movie, speaks volumes about the quality of life. It also speaks of how we want to die.

You are definitely in the minority if you haven't talked about how you want to die in the last week. The controversy swirling around Florida's Terri Schiavo has the issue leading every newscast and coffee room discussion in the country.

As is always the case with such high-profile topics, the humanity has rapidly gotten lost in the posturing of those involved in the debate.

It is a travesty that members of Congress, even the president, have decided that they must weigh in on whether Schiavo should continue on life support or allow nature to take its course. It shames me that some of my conservative Christian brethren feel compelled to turn this into a right-to-life matter, somehow relating Schiavo's fate to the debate over abortion.

It is a tragedy that Michael Schiavo and Terri's parents have felt compelled to battle for the last decade and more over what Terri would have wanted. The only winners in this situation, if there can be such a thing, are the care facilities that have profited from keeping Terri alive.

Sadly, the decision over Terri's fate is 15 years overdue. It shouldn't be about removing a feeding tube – it should have been about putting the feeding tube in in the first place.

It makes ultimate sense to me that removal of a feeding tube or unplugging a respirator is an action that directly leads to a person's death. The fact it is an action makes it wrong, at least in my book.

But, and this is a big but, if the person involved has requested not to live as a vegetable, it makes sense to me not to take the "life-saving" action in the first place. It is my choice, because the "life" Terri Schiavo is experiencing is not what I would consider to be life.

We here at the Gazette have firsthand experience in this matter. More than three years ago, our longtime receptionist, Karen Thomason, suffered a heart attack and a series of strokes that left her in the same type of severely brain-damaged state Schiavo is in. There was hope early on that Karen could recover. She appeared to respond to her surroundings – smiling, grimacing, moving her head.

She didn't have a living will, and her actions gave those around her some hope. Doctors were hesitant to crush those hopes, so they couched their comments with vague possibilities. Family members decided they couldn't pull the plug.

Today, Karen lies in a "rehabilitation" hospital, feeding tube still in place. She still opens her eyes, and moves. Rather, her body does that. I don't think Karen does. I don't think that Karen is there. But her body will keep ticking, likely until it dies of old age.

Terri Schiavo was 26 years old when she was stricken. That's clearly not an age when you're thinking about how you want to die – or whether you should have that option. You see, just because I don't want extraordinary steps to be taken to keep my body alive, I think there's a reason those technologies exist, and I think people should have the right to use them.

Bottom line, I'm begging, pleading with you to decide how you want to die and put it in writing. It's called a living will, and there is a plethora of assistance out there in getting one done. In California, you don't even have to have it notarized to make it binding.

Don't make those around you suffer with the indecision. Tell them.

Say: "This is a good way to die."

STORIES IN THE NEWS

PUBLIC SURVEILLANCE CAMERAS burst on the scene after 9-11, and became ever more prevalent as their price went down and the price of police went up. This was my position in 2005; I can't say I feel exactly the same today.

Sept. 15, 2012

I need to pick a bone with the editorial this week – which, at first glance, would seem to be a silly thing to do, since I wrote the editorial.

But the editorial is the newspaper's opinion, while this column is my opinion. The difference may be subtle, but it is real.

There's also a huge difference between what is written on this page – opinion – and the news stories in the rest of the paper. Those differences seem to escape some (see the letters in "Our Mailbox"), but that is fodder for a different column.

I agree, reluctantly, with the concept that there needs to be more police presence, more deterrence, in our increasingly violent home town. I agree, less reluctantly, that we have to do whatever it takes to protect the vast majority of our city's youth from the small minority seemingly determined to spread mayhem, with no regard for responsibility or authority.

What I disagree with is the path that this approach puts this city on. The ongoing emphasis on deterrence will lead to, has already led to, a government ready and willing to put cameras on the street corners where it can't afford to station police officers. It is a running start toward the slippery slope of eliminating civil rights for all in the effort to stop a few.

A day I had long feared arrived last week. That was when a City Council member, in all sincerity and not even hesitating, said, "If people aren't doing anything wrong, then they don't have anything to worry about."

The same council member laughed when a colleague suggested Long Beach was taking a step toward George Orwell's

"1984" or worse, Aldous Huxley's "Brave New World." This isn't a laughing matter.

More disheartening was Mayor Beverly O'Neill's support for the camera proposal. She was right when she cited figures showing a precipitous drop in crime where cameras were installed, and her logic that these dangerous times called for **extreme measures** made sense.

But I'm not sure I'm ready to pay the price required – my freedom from government surveillance. I'm definitely not ready to let Val Lerch or anyone else decide whether what I'm doing is "wrong" or not.

I didn't fight against red light cameras because they are designed specifically to capture wrong-doing. I don't have a problem with in-store surveillance cameras aimed at cash registers for much the same reason (although it's more than a little disconcerting to know that every grocery store I go to can track how often I buy donuts, thanks to those ubiquitous discount cards).

But when Big Brother starts watching as I walk down a street, can his intrusion into my workplace, my home, be far behind?

After all, what would be wrong with that? If I wasn't doing anything wrong, I wouldn't have anything to worry about, right?

Surely no government in their right mind would decide it was wrong to read "Animal Farm," or the "Kama Sutra," would they? Nah.

Still, I have to wonder whether the price we are paying for our safety today might be our freedom in the future.

And forgive me again if I say that it seems possible to me that price might just be too high.

STORIES IN THE NEWS

THE INAUGURATION OF the first non-white President of the United States signified a true milestone in our country's history. It was a thrill to write this one.

Jan. 21, 2009

I'm writing this on Tuesday morning, just as I have pretty much every week for the last 17 years.

But I can't ignore the fact that this Tuesday is different. Barack Obama's inauguration isn't just reaching across the country, it's reaching across the world.

It would be naïve to think that everyone in America, let alone the world, is thrilled to call Obama Mr. President. Beyond the sad few who still decry the election of a black man, there are legitimate differences with policy and concern about lack of experience.

Still, there is a greater sense of anticipation attached to this new president than any I personally have experienced. (I've been around for a long time, but I was still in elementary school when John Kennedy became president.)

I do not mean to minimalize the historic significance of the election of a man of color. It is a huge barrier to overcome, and I'm glad it is over.

But I think the more important issue here is the chance for a new start. I can't remember a time when we needed a new start more.

Obama promised change throughout his campaign, and change long has been the clarion call of any politician trying to overcome the establishment. We the people have a predilection for change, as well. If it isn't a matter of throw the bums out, it's always exciting to have something new.

And boy, do we need something new.

Obama has pushed a major economic recovery package, hopefully passed as early as next week. But this package won't just be handouts to keep banks and Wall Street afloat; it is expected to generate jobs by changing our approach to everything from energy production to transportation.

It is no exaggeration to say the entire free world is watching and hoping as Obama takes office. Can he really extricate us from the quagmire of Iraq? Can he find a way to actually resolve the struggle in Afghanistan? Is there any chance he can help make progress in the Middle East?

Well, there is change, so there is hope.

By the way, I hope the world paid attention to how power changes hands today. It wasn't a military coup, or palace intrigue. It was the will of the people.

Millions, no, billions of people stopped today to watch a man take an oath. Millions, no, billions of people joined in prayer with the hope that that man can lead our country to a brighter future.

Thank God it is more than one man who will ultimately do the work. I can't imagine the pressure Obama must feel. Instead, it is a nation seeking change – change for the good.

Sound sappy? Sure, I admit it. But that's the feeling that this morning is sparking in me as I type while watching the celebration.

To create change, you have to have hope. And today, I have hope.

STORIES IN THE NEWS

THE DEMISE OF daily newspapers was a sad hallmark of the first decade of the 21st Century. Every closure struck a blow in my industry. When it hit my hometown, I had to talk about it.

May 13, 2009

I think I know how workers for Chrysler, GM and Ford feel now.

Congress has been conducting hearings about the imminent demise of newspapers as we know them today. There has been lots of talk on that subject over the last year or two, with plenty of justification.

Back in Colorado, I was always a Denver Post reader. But it was a requirement to see what the Rocky (the Rocky Mountain News) had to say on big stories, and the Rocky was the better regional and statewide paper of the two.

Now the Rocky is no more. And it is far from the only daily to fold in the last few years.

The shrinking Press-Telegram, both physically and in staff, is an ongoing concern in Long Beach. As much as I dearly love to beat them to stories or at least write better stories than they offer, I will be the first to say our city needs a good daily paper it can call its own.

But maybe I'm just being a stubborn dinosaur, unwilling to give up on an anachronistic form of information dissemination. Perhaps I ought to be concentrating on getting our Web site even more dynamic, or spending hours on Facebook, or trying to sell people on reading us on a Kindle.

I admit to posting a story on www.gazettes.com last week, three days before it hit the street in our Uptown and Downtown Gazettes. I was the first to physically report that hotel workers were suing the Hyatt Long Beach. The P-T had it in print on Saturday, but I had it in the ether on Friday.

Big deal, huh?

The physical gathering of information we call journalism is

the key to any news enterprise. As far as I know, no one is arguing that there isn't a continuing and growing need for that process. One person testifying before Congress warned that, without the survival of newspapers and the type of journalism they provide, it will soon become a boom time for local and state political corruption. Why? Because no one with any credibility will be watching.

How we disseminate information is the real debate today. It costs money to collect news and to write it in a coherent manner. In other words, for some strange reason my colleagues and I would like to be paid for our work, and we'd like to have adequate tools to do that work.

Let me suggest that, at least when it comes to community papers like the Grunion, our existence does more than provide a good place to decide what to do next weekend, or to find out what silly thing our City Council wants to do. I'm talking about the very advertisers we count on for our survival.

On a good week, there are a couple hundred ads in the Grunion; more than a hundred in the Downtown and Uptown. Each of those advertisers is trying to let potential customers know about their services, whether it's a good meal or a root canal. It's a rare outfit that can prosper strictly on its current customers and a little word of mouth. Most business owners rely on getting their message out in order to stay in business.

Does it make sense for our locally-owned businesses to advertise on Google or Yahoo? Would it make sense for us to find a way to cram 200 or so ads on our Web site and expect you to look at them all?

I think not.

I could go on about our personalized service to classified advertisers, and the virtual guarantee that those who advertise with us are legitimate. That's a tad different than the generic list Web sites.

Instead, I'll just say that our very existence provides a service to our community. Of course, we try to do much more, and I personally am very proud of the job we do.

Now it's up to you. Keep reading, please.

Thank you.

THE RECESSION OF 2008, combined with the rapidly changing media environment, caused huge upheaval in our industry – a serious double whammy. When a writer decided to go back to school, I found out just how serious it was.

June 5, 2009

> I knew it was bad, but I didn't think it was this bad.
> My ignorance, I suppose, comes from the fact that I have a job. I've been able to shake my head about the state of the job market, then go deposit my paycheck.
> My awakening occurred late last week.
> I am in possession of one of today's most precious commodities – a vacant position. I'm not real happy about that, because it means I'm losing one of my stars.
> I don't think I chased Kelly Garrison away; at least she didn't say it was me specifically. Fact is, she's going back to graduate school after a two-year stint here as features editor and web master (I kept lobbying for web mistress, but the HR department said it was sexual harassment).
> She's going to be missed. She has been an integral part of our team, and in particular can take credit for getting our nifty new website up to speed.
> Rather than replace her, I decided to start over with an entry-level position. It's graduation season, so I figured I'd get at least a few applicants to choose from.
> So far, I've received 163 resumes. That's in three days.
> Credit the wonder of the Internet for part of that. Mine has been more than a nationwide search; it has stretched around the globe. I've received resumes from Shanghai, Australia, Europe and Africa. That's only slightly more mind-boggling than the resumes from Oregon to Ohio, from Texas to New York.
> I thought I'd be looking at new college graduates seeking to start their careers. There were plenty of those. But there also were

people graduating with master's degrees — and from schools like the Columbia School of Journalism and USC's own Annenberg School of Journalism.

There also have been more than three dozen applicants with significant professional experience in journalism. I'm talking about full-timers, not just freelance, and I'm talking years, not months.

I'm interviewing a few of those folks. I've made it clear that we're talking about entry-level pay here, not the type of salary their experience might have commanded five years ago.

They don't blink. Apparently, something is better than nothing in this market.

And where does that lead the truly entry-level reporter? I shudder to think.

Of course, there also is the passion for journalism. For those of us with ink in our veins, there's nothing quite as painful as not having the chance to write on a regular basis.

I'm trying to look on the bright side here. Assuming I'm able to do my job as an interviewer, the Gazettes will get an extremely talented, qualified new writer.

But that leaves 162 (and counting) people out in the cold, still looking. That's the dark side of this equation. Can you imagine how much talent is going to waste among those I don't hire? Let alone the personal stories of each journalist looking for, and not finding, at least here, a job?

It seems I'm writing more and more often about the hard times being inflicted on people by this economy these days — just look at the editorial above. But this hiring process has smacked me in the face with the magnitude of the situation. I know part of it is my particular industry, but still.

The economy will eventually turn around, I know. And I hope and pray that those young (or not so young) journalists I turn away won't give up their dreams. I wish I could hire you all.

Keep trying. We need you.

AMERICA'S LONG INVOLVEMENT in Iraq marred much of a decade, and impacted a generation. Early on, patriotism was easy to talk about. It wasn't so easy eight years after the fact. But I tried.

July 1, 2009

There were fireworks – real fireworks, not mortars and rockets – in Iraq last Tuesday.

It's hard to picture a better way to prepare for Independence Day in the U.S. of A.

I know, this is far from the end of our country's long involvement in Iraq. The fact the Iraqi government declared June 30 a national holiday as American troops pulled out of cities and towns did little to alter the competing, and sobering, fact that there are 130,000 troops still in-country.

Nor does it mean that the violence will stop – it has in fact increased as the deadline to end physical American authority neared. Still, we are turning over much of the country to freely chosen leaders. That's reason to celebrate.

As the father of a Marine (okay, stepfather, but now's not the time to quibble), I am painfully aware that plenty of danger remains in Iraq, Afghanistan, Pakistan and other parts of the world. But it is feeling a lot more like we're doing the right thing lately. That's reason to celebrate.

My father fought in Korea and I grew up in the heat and turmoil of the Vietnam War. I am of the generation that suddenly realized the America is not always destined to win, and might in fact make a mistake or two. And wonder of wonders, we were allowed to say that without getting thrown into jail (at least most of the time) or shipped off to Siberia. That's reason to celebrate.

I believe in saying "in God we trust," and I have a tendency to pray that this country be watched over and guided on a path of righteousness. I stop well short of believing we are a chosen people, though, and take every chance to seek worldly solutions to worldly problems. I'm free to both worship and disagree. That's reason to celebrate.

You won't find an "America, Love It or Leave It" bumper sticker anywhere near my car. I'm of the "let's make our country better" frame of mind. But I still get a lump in my throat when I hear "The Star-Spangle Banner" (at least most versions). That's reason to celebrate.

I am proud to be an American. Most of the time, I am proud of what Americans are trying to do overseas. I do believe that we are in Iraq, Afghanistan and the rest not just to protect our own interests, but to help the people there, too. I'm not so naïve as to think that all of our government's motives are pure, but I persist in the notion that the men and women both on the ground and in the command office are trying to do the right thing. That's a reason to celebrate.

I can write this column and talk about patriotism. You can write back and disagree. Neither one of us is going to be persecuted by a government saying only one way of thinking is allowed. That's reason to celebrate.

My patriotism isn't something I wear on my sleeve. I hope I don't take being an American for granted. I do believe that it is far better than the alternative, however. That's reason to celebrate.

These are difficult times for many. Being American, we can at least try to make it better, and I think most of us make that effort both here and abroad. And that truly is reason to celebrate.

Happy Fourth of July.

A POOR COUNTRY already in trouble, Haiti's devastating earthquake touched hearts in the U.S., and Long Beach. I rarely failed to address such world news.

Jan. 20, 2010

What can I say?

I certainly can't avoid it. Last week's earthquake in Haiti is in the running to become the worst natural disaster of this century, at least in terms of death toll. It's likely there never will be an exact number, but it's clear the total will be in six figures. It could rival the number of deaths caused by the 2004 Indonesian earthquake and tsunami, which killed 230,000 over a wide area including Sri Lanka, Thailand, India and the Maldives.

We've had Hurricane Katrina in the United States, and the damage there was spread over a wide area, as well. The disaster in New Orleans is well-documented and still being repaired.

But Haiti is different. This is yet another disaster in a series of disasters – the country was still recovering from a series of hurricanes in 2008. Haiti has been racked by political turmoil for decades, and is one of the poorest countries in the world.

What can I say?

The pictures of devastation are everywhere. People are suffering from lack of water and food to the point where the death toll of the aftermath is going to be significant.

The entire world, but especially the United States, has mobilized to provide aid. More help than Haiti has seen in the past decade will land at the airport in January.

But as of this writing on Tuesday, it has been a week since the earthquake struck, and help is barely reaching the main Port-au-Prince population centers, let alone the outskirts of the capitol.

Sadly, the almost inevitable looting and rioting has begun. As desperate people seek food and water, others seek any excuse to take what the want.

What can I say?

I stuck my toe in the social network this week and asked that question on Facebook. Here are a couple of the suggestions I received.

How about, "Something about not giving in to compassion fatigue? How to participate locally."

Or to get a little more personal, there's this:

"Perhaps instructions or guidance on how to adopt the orphaned. Would that help? I have a loving home, a huge heart and would love to cherish and raise a child."

I'm sure there will be more suggestions as time goes on. If there's one thing that can be said for humanity as a whole, it is that they respond with charity and zeal when a disaster strikes.

What can I say?

Can I say I'll give money? Not really – I don't have it to give. Can I say I'll give time to go help? No, I don't have the wherewithal to pick up and leave, even if I did have the skills they actually need down there.

Can I say I'll pack up blankets, shoes and clothes to ship to Haiti? I would, but every relief agency in the world says not to do that, at least right now. I'd ship food and water if I could do so in significant quantities. But I can't.

What I can say is that I'll pray. And I'll beg those who can help to help, and I'll promise to support those efforts in whatever way I can.

I can say that a disaster like this makes me realize how lucky I am, and how precious every moment of life can be. It can all be gone in a heartbeat.

What can I say? I'm sorry I can't say, and do, more.

HOW DO YOU react when a sworn enemy is killed? It was a question on many people's minds when Osama bin Laden was confirmed killed.

May 5, 2011

This Sunday is Mother's Day, and I should be writing an ode to mothers everywhere.

It's even more important this year because both my daughter-in-law and one of my stepdaughters qualify as mothers-to-be. That makes Maria a grandmother-to-be (again). And I, more than most, acknowledge the importance of mothers everywhere to the continuation of civilization as we know it.

But Osama bin Laden was killed on Sunday.

That's the only place you are going to see that statement in this paper. It's not that I am oblivious to the importance of this development – quite the contrary. I have, just like you, been watching the news with fascination, monitoring the response on television and online.

I'm not real sure I have a lot to add to the cacophony. I somehow doubt that Long Beach is turning to us as their primary source of information on the how and why of the operation that ended the terrorist's life, or the reaction of governments and 9-11 victims to his demise.

Coverage of such international events simply is not part of our mission as a community news source. But I can't ignore it totally. So, with apologies to mothers everywhere, I'm using this space to offer a few thoughts.

You are hearing plenty of people saying they are happy that bin Laden is dead. Clearly it is a just end to a man who publicly advocated and celebrated the death of others.

There's also an undeniable sigh of collective relief amongst those responsible for this country's security. It is hard to deny that Americans were at risk from bin Laden's malevolent attention, and we have to be a tad safer with one less enemy in the world today.

But, and I think this is a pretty big but, I squirmed uncomfortably as I watched the crowd in front of the White House chanting "USA, USA" and waving American flags. The images were far too similar to those scenes a decade ago in some Arabian countries, celebrating the blow against America.

Those images back then sparked outrage that a people, any people, could celebrate the death of innocents. Of course, that's the difference, right? Americans are celebrating the death of a self-proclaimed enemy, a man responsible for literally thousands of deaths. That makes all the difference, right? Right?

Somehow, I don't think so. A rally that has all the earmarks of a city whose team has just won the Super Bowl doesn't seem fitting, even in this situation.

I saw another image on television I thought much more appropriate – the image of the simple memorial in Pennsylvania to the passengers on Flight 93, and one person there, praying. It was a picture of someone remembering the victims, not celebrating vengeance.

Don't get me wrong. I am glad bin Laden is dead, and pleased that it was American troops providing the coup de grace. I am sorry that it took so long to get it done.

I guess I'd just like to see a little more solemnity, a little more class for lack of a better word, in the completion of this task. I prefer the John Wayne or the Jimmy Stewart approach, if you know what I mean.

Sadly, the death of bin Laden does not mean the end of terrorism. It doesn't even mean we can march triumphantly out of Iraq or Afghanistan. We need to continue our vigilance, and we should be prepared to fight the good fight whenever necessary.

I'm ready to do that. But I'd like to do it, I'd like my country to do it, with a bit of dignity and a lot of respect for the seriousness of the situation.

After all, that's what my mother taught me to do.

A HORRIFIC SHOOTING in neighboring Seal Beach – the Salon Meritage murders – made national news, and caused me to reach outside our city to cover a breaking news story. It caused me to revisit how and when newspapers cover tragedy. I was honestly interested in illiciting comments, but I fear the column was too close to the tragedy for that sort of dispassionate debate.

Oct. 27, 2011

What would you do if you had my job?

More specifically, what would you put in the paper if you had the power to decide?

I'm truly interested. I've asked this question many times in the past, in many different ways. We've done polls, we've asked focus groups, we've pleaded for opinions just like I'm pleading now.

For the most part, people don't respond. And when they do, they offer answers that show what they'd like to think they want, not what they really want.

Newspapers aren't the only ones with this problem. Ask a decent cross-section of people what they watch on television, and they'll tell you it's educational programming, documentaries, etc. Of course, when the Nielsen machine gets hooked up to their 55" plasma screen, it's cops and robbers, sitcoms with lots of sexual innuendo, "Dancing With The Stars," "Wipeout," "1,000 Ways To Die" and maybe, just maybe, a cooking show.

I go through this self-examination about the content of our Gazettes pretty frequently. Truth be told, it's one of the favorite topics whenever a couple of news people get together.

When something like the tragic Seal Beach shooting takes place, that ratchets up the conversation considerably. How much information is enough? When does it cease being news and begin being morbid curiosity?

The community wants to know what happened, who it happened to and quite often, what they can do about it. It's our job to provide that information.

But does that include knocking on the door of victims' families? Does it include television cameras at church services? Different news people make different decisions.

I'm sure you've heard the old newspaper cliché, "If it bleeds, it leads." It's the concept that news is only news when it is sensational, or shocking. Dog bites man isn't news; man bites dog is big news.

I've lost track of the times that I've been told newspapers need to print more good news. Frankly, at the Gazette we don't get that as much as some papers, because we print plenty of good news about our schools, our children, our nonprofits and more. That's part of being a community newspaper, and we believe in it.

But there is the issue of who is reading all that good news, and who is reading all that stuff about crime, violence and corruption. And sad to say, experience has shown that more people read that shocking stuff, that intrusive stuff, than those interested in the youngster who has overcome adversity.

Our website has this nifty program that tells us how many people read what stories when – another marvel of the electronic age. I refuse to base my decisions solely on those numbers, at least partially because I'm really old and don't trust these new-fangled things.

But I have to acknowledge the trend – at least on line, more people read the crime stories than read this column (more people read the classified ads than read this column, too).

I feel good about our level of coverage in regards to the Seal Beach shooting. But I also understand the head-to-toe, top-to-bottom coverage seen on television and in daily newspapers. People watch it, people read it. And if there's one thing that mainstream media has learned to do well, it is giving people what they want.

I, we, think you want something different from the *Gazette*. We've long considered community news our bread and butter, and that isn't going to change. I believe you want to, need to, know what your government is doing for and to you, and you want to, need to, know what your kids and your neighbors are up to.

But it would be foolish to pretend that the community doesn't change too, so I'm asking. What would you do?

STORIES IN THE NEWS

THE SEXUAL ABUSE scandal that rocked Penn State tarnished the legacy of a true hero of college football, Joe Paterno. When I tried to suggest Paterno had made a mistake that would forever scar him, but shouldn't negate everything he did, I heard a howl of protest that I was defending Paterno. You decide.

Nov. 17, 2011

It's a matter of trust.

We trust that people in a position of authority will do the right thing. That trust is pretty much all we have to keep making our democratic society work. In some ways, I suppose that it's pretty surprising that it works as well as it does.

You can tell how much value we put in that trust by the way we react when it is violated. That's what happened last week in Happy Valley, Pennsylvania. It's also why a story about a football coach has dominated the news for the last week.

This violation of trust involves one of the most basic trusts — that of our children. It is what makes this situation so volatile, so emotional.

One of the first, and most difficult, decisions parents face is trusting our children with coaches when they become involved in sports. We count on those coaches to not just teach the sport, but the character traits that make team sports such an important part of growing up.

We learn cooperation, sacrifice for the greater good, sharing, surviving failure, depending on others and so much more by being a part of a team. Most youngsters look to their coach to model those traits.

Which makes it just that much worse when that trust is betrayed.

It's very true that Jerry Sandusky still hasn't had his day in court to face accusations of sexually molesting young boys visiting the Penn State football program. And it is clearly true that Joe Paterno has done immeasurable good for many in his decades as head coach of the Nittany Lions.

The grand jury testimony is damning, though, and university officials have taken decisive action. The venerable Paterno's lack of protest after being summarily dismissed seems by many to be an acknowledgement that he did not do enough to stop and/or report Sandusky's activities.

In a few short days, a legacy that has taken decades to build has been destroyed.

Is that fair? Maybe not. But it is certainly understandable.

I'll leave Sandusky alone to suffer his own fate. People who do what he is accused of doing are the lowest of the low in my opinion (and apparently in much of our society's opinion) and he will face justice.

I'm more interested in Paterno's fate, motivations and feelings. Here is a man who, by all accounts, focused on doing the right thing for most of his long life. His reputation has been gained for making sure his players stayed out of trouble and in school, with most graduating, as much as it is for building a winning program.

So how could someone with such moral fiber soft-pedal some of the direct allegations brought to his attention? What went through his mind when he told his athletic director there were reports of "something of a sexual nature," then failed to do anything more?

I can only assume that Paterno willingly ignored something he didn't want to believe. Most of us have faced the same sort of situation – a loved one in the grip of an addiction, a child doing the wrong thing, a subordinate (or superior) engaged in nefarious activity. I know there have been times when I've ignored something largely because I didn't want to believe it.

Have I done that to the detriment of others? Maybe so.

Have I ever betrayed another's trust? Sadly, yes.

Damned right.

It takes decades to repair that sort of damage. I'd like to think that today, I do the right thing, and that makes a difference. That's really all I can do.

Joe Paterno doesn't have decades. There is little he can do to take the tarnish away. I feel sorry for him.

But he was wrong. A position of trust requires the right thing be done. Every time.

That doesn't change.

Part THREE
About The Life I Lead

ABOUT THE LIFE I LEAD

I COULDN'T VERY well leave out the first column of 20 years of Salt, now could I? It was far from my best writing, but it did seem to manage to introduce what I hoped to do with the column, and the paper.

April 23, 1992

So just what is this Grunion thing, anyway?

I had heard about Grunion, I think, during my formative days in Colorado. They were some kind of fish that did a lemming-like thing on the beach, I thought.

I had to – I was going to work for something called the Grunion Gazette, and it seemed incumbent on me to at least know what the namesake looked like.

To be honest I still haven't seen a Grunion up close and personal. I expect to remedy that some time this summer.

But I can tell you that they are fish with the rather strange behavior of coming to the beach to mate. The female Grunion drills herself in the sand to lay up to 3,000 eggs while the male wraps himself around her and, well, does what male fish do.

All this in 30 seconds. Then they try to get back into the water before they asphyxiate in the air.

Humans being what they are, grabbing the fish before they make it back to the ocean is a popular pastime. I won't make a judgment; I've been known to hook a trout or two in my time.

But I do know that people turn to the Gazette to find out when they can head for the beach to try to catch me little buggers.

And I can tell you that the season is closed through May. When it opens again in June, we'll be running the traditional Grunion Run boxes again.

All of this is a round-about way of telling you, the reader, that I am new to the area. I've taken over from a community fixture in Joe Ponepinto. Joe developed a quality paper during his tenure – I hope to build on that.

But to do so, I need your help. If there is something going on that I should know about, give me a call. If 1 get something wrong in a story, let me know, so I don't do it again.

I also need your patience. Explain it all — what you've known for years is brand new to me.

In return, I promise to give you a listening ear. This is a community paper, and I'm interested in the community.

I also promise to let you learn about me as I learn about you. This space, at least for awhile, will be dedicated to the musings and adventures of a transplant to Long Beach. When you get tired of it, let me know.

So just what is this Harry Saltzgaver thing, anyway?

We'll start next week.

ABOUT THE LIFE I LEAD

IT SEEMS IRONIC now to be writing about a layoff as a major life event. But it surely was then, just as every layoff since 2008 has been a big deal for someone.

I have to admit, this probably was written at least with a small hope someone would see it and offer Reetz a job. It didn't work, but she did get another job, and still has it today. Too bad that isn't true for everyone.

Oct. 14, 1993

> Reetz and I became a statistic last week.
> She was laid off. Lost her job. Position eliminated.
> We're one of the lucky ones. I've still got a job. She's talented, versatile, with skills in demand even in today's tough job market. She's already been on one call-back interview, and I'm confident she'll be back to work soon.
> But that doesn't make it any less painful.
> It hurts when someone says you're no longer needed, even when they're wrong. It hurts when the boss hands you your walking papers, even if she's crying when she does it.
> In Reetz's case, the import-export firm she worked for is consolidating – there's still a recession out there. The executives and sales force now will be forced to go it alone, without administrative support. The firm's cutting its own throat to save a few bucks, and in the back of their minds, they know it.
> But that doesn't make it any less painful.
> A layoff is a particularly nasty way to lose a job. At least when you're fired, there's a concrete reason – even if you disagree with the reason. There's the cause and effect of "you did this (or at least we think you did), you didn't do that, so now you don't have a job."
> With a layoff, the concrete reason is nebulous. It's "the company needs to cut back," or "we don't have enough work any more." No reflection on your personal abilities, right?
> But that doesn't make it any less painful.

When your job's eliminated, it strikes to the core of your self-confidence. Reetz knows she's very good at what she does. I tell her so. Her bosses told her so, in writing and in person.

Still, getting laid off means you aren't indispensable. Someone at least thinks they can get along without you. No matter how confident you are, that's a blow.

Glowing references, phrases like "I wish we could keep you," and "we'll bring you back if we can" are intended to help keep layoffs from reflecting on personal ability. That doesn't change the fact you're holding a severance check, and a box to clean out your desk, though.

It doesn't make it any less painful.

Our production-oriented society has long forced people to equate their worth as individuals with the job they do. It's an erroneous perception. Reetz is worth more than any paycheck. So are the thousands and hundreds of thousands who have lost their jobs in recent years through no fault of their own.

We'll bounce back. Always have, always will. Reetz will take this opportunity and find an even better job. Always has, always will. It's one of the things I love about her.

But for now, we're a statistic.

And it's painful.

ABOUT THE LIFE I LEAD

BEING A MEMBER of my family has proven a bit embarrassing at times. Then there were the times I wrote about the family members, too. I think Alex has been the topic of more columns than any other single subject except, perhaps, my faith. This is a pretty good example.

Feb. 13, 1997

My son, Alex, officially becomes a man Monday.

He turns 18. He reaches a majority (something to do with calling kids minors, I guess). He's eligible to vote, and he has to register with the Selective Service.

It's an arbitrary milestone, just like any other birthday. I suspect he probably thought his 16th was more important, because he got to start driving then.

But for Dad, it's the biggie.

Back when I turned 18, we had just won the vote – largely based on the fact that we were expected to go out and get shot at in Vietnam when we were 18. Thank God there's no need for the draft, at least right now.

It was a different world then. I suspect, though, that my dad had a few thoughts on my 18th birthday, as well.

I'm more fortunate than most. I can look at a young man ready to join the world and make a positive difference. He's bright, caring and enjoys life.

I wish I could take more credit for that. But the fact is, he was raised in a single-parent household – and I wasn't that parent.

Alex's mom and I split up when he was 2. No need to go into the details. Suffice it to say his second birthday party was one of the hardest events to attend I've every experienced.

But again, I was fortunate. It wasn't an acrimonious split, and both of us agreed that Alex's welfare was paramount. I remained – and remain – a part of his life.

I lived within 100 miles of them until Alex started school – within a few hundred until he got into high school. I saw him as often as possible; include a couple of full summer stays.

I have paid child support for 16 years, never missing a month and never being more than a week late. And yes, I get very upset at people who don't take the concept of supporting a child seriously.

But it's the things I haven't done that come to mind today. I didn't hold his hand in the hospital when he had his tonsils out. I didn't get to see him start his first high school baseball game. I didn't help him pick out his first car (even if I did help pay for it).

The birds and the bees talk, such as it was, came way too late, and over the telephone. The help with homework consisted of suggesting a few books. I started him skiing, but I've never been on more than an intermediate run with him (he's a black diamond, extreme sort of guy now).

I like to think —no, I know — I've been a part of Alex's upbringing. I just wish I had been more of a part.

I'm damned proud of my boy — and his mother. They took a less than ideal situation and made it not just work, but succeed. Congratulations, Eloise. You did good.

And Alex, I love you. You're everything and more I ever hoped you would be.

Happy birthday.

ABOUT THE LIFE I LEAD

TIME, AND CHANGING social mores, seem to accelerate as I grow older. Time speeding up is admittedly a matter of perception. The speeding up of change in social mores, however, is a documented fact.

It seemed fair to me to try to explore those changes as they impacted my life. Alex helped with that often.

March 26, 1998

I woke up the other morning with five college kids asleep in my living room.

Talk about generation gap. I knew I was getting older, but Alex (my son) and his friends from the University of Colorado pounded the fact home.

That's the bad news. The good news is that the next generation is going to do just fine, thank you. At least that's my take if this bunch of young adults is representative, and I think they are.

Alex and his friends are on spring break. This isn't the spring break of MTV or Lake Havasu, or Fort Lauderdale. This is a group of college freshmen taking a trip to have a little innocent fun.

No booze (they're 19 or 20, and smart enough to know better), no drugs (ditto), but quite a bit of what passes for rock 'n' roll these days. They are almost scary with the amount of responsibility they take, but manage to do the little things that show they're still kids.

Responsibility – and sensitivity – example number one. The rest of the gang decided to go do something else on Sunday so Alex and I could spend the day alone.

I don't know if I can express what that meant to me. Alex's mom and I divorced when he was 2 years old, and it seems like we've spent the last 17 years trying to steal a whole day together.

We didn't do anything extra special – played a round of golf, watched the Broncos Super Bowl video, at pizza. He tried to convince me to buy a plant (I decline; I kill green things).

It's a day I'll cherish.

Example two. When I left for work Monday morning, the condo looked like a tornado had just hit. I scheduled at least two hours for cleanup that evening.

But when I opened the door Monday night, the place was clean (well, sort of). Beds were made, dishes put away. I was beginning to worry that Alex and his friends were some sort of Stepford college students.

Then I found the glass and bowl out on the balcony. And the towel wadded up in the bathroom. All is well in almost adulthood land.

When I think back to my college days of ducking parents to party hardy, of dishes with mold and glasses thrown away because they'd never be clean again, I feel a sense of shame. And of pride. I survived, and my son is doing it better than I.

I've deliberately left the most telling of the generation gap signs for last, mainly because I'm not too sure how you, gentle reader, will react. You see, the fivesome sprawled around my living room consisted of three girls and two guys.

Before you go screaming into the night, remember that all five are adults, despite the fact that they look like high school kids to me. And remember I was in college during the flower power days, when sex was on top of the list of sex, drugs and rock and roll.

Truth is, it was a valuable lesson for me in just how responsible, sensible and relaxed with themselves my progeny and his friends have become. Co-ed sleeping arrangements were no big deal. It was a night's sleep before a drive to San Diego, not a college orgy. I can't say the same would have been true 25 years ago.

I have no doubt these kids will make mistakes, do things they'll regret later, and maybe do things I wouldn't approve of. But I can't shake the feeling that they are better prepared for adulthood than I was at their age.

Did I mention that I'm proud?

ABOUT THE LIFE I LEAD

I GREATLY ADMIRE the "slice of life" style of writing, and have attempted its execution many times. It is one of the best ways I've found to share how I was feeling at that point in time.

And it often offers the opportunity for a little humor, too.

Jan. 7, 1999

7:10 a.m. Jan. 2, 1999 – On the first tee at Recreation Park Golf Course (Big Rec to regulars).

It had been a cool night, and the ground fog filled the swale that is the 14th hole's signature. Tendrils of mist rose from that ephemeral pond, ready to meet the rising sun. In the sky, wispy clouds dotted the eastern horizon.

As the first gold-dusted edge of the sun struggled toward those clouds, I positioned myself so the stately palm trees bordering the course framed the sight. Willows, eucalyptus and myriad other trees were backlit by the first rays of light.

Slowly, hues of burnt gold and royal purple painted the wandering clouds. The ground fog vibrated in sympathy, becoming a watercolor rainbow.

As the sun surfaced, it provided its own course in color changing. Beginning as a huge orange disk, it transformed itself. As it reduced in size, at least in my eyes, its color brightened and intensified, quickly becoming a shimmering yellow. As I watched, it ducked behind a passing cloud to change once again, returning as an incandescent white, showering the landscaped with light and warmth.

I turned, and hit my first shot out of bounds.

No, this is not my entry in the most hyperbolic writing contest of the year. Yes, it is a true story. And yes, I managed to grasp a bit of the symbolism of the experience.

I've lived in Southern California for more than seven years now, and still find myself continually amazed by the idyllic weather we enjoy, particularly in the winter. It doesn't hurt the comparison when the national news is full of the "Storm of '99" paralyzing the eastern half of the country.

I know, I know. It's not all sweetness and light out here in Lotus Land. We have our earthquakes, our brush fires, our mudslides. For those who look beyond the immediate, this long stretch of sunny skies and warm temperatures foretell water shortages if it doesn't start raining soon.

But, for a change, I didn't let "the big picture" overwhelm the bigger picture I was seeing. Instead of thinking, as is my normal modus operandi, I actually let the moment take me.

I've experienced a few similar sunrises, at least in terms of impact. There was one as I sat on the shoulder of one of my beloved Colorado mountains. There was another, way back in college, rising above a natural duck pond on the plains of the same state.

Funny, but most of the "biggy" sunrises seem to happen at our near the first of the year. And, although it likely is a matter of seeing the past through rose-colored glasses, it seems to me that the years I experienced killer sunrises like this always turned out well.

I get that feeling about 1999. It's going to be a very good year.

I hope you saw the same sunrise.

ABOUT THE LIFE I LEAD

BEING A FATHER is one of the hardest, and most important, jobs I can think of. It's certainly worth writing about – particularly when the son teaches the father a lesson.

April 27, 2000

Giving advice is almost always a mistake. Giving advice to a 21-year-old son can be deadly.

There is good news from Colorado, where my son, Alex, is finishing up his junior year in college. As a business major, it was critical that he land an internship this coming summer.

He pulled it off in fine fashion, receiving not one, but two offers. He has the chance to go to work for AT&T for the summer, or work for the Colorado Golf Association.

Guess which one Dad suggested. Now guess which one Alex took.

Being able to put communications giant AT&T on a resume is pure gold. With a summer's experience there, it is a sure bet the corporate recruiters would be knocking on Alex's door when he graduates a year from now.

Alex listened to that. He even gave it some thought, I believe. Then he gave me his answer.

"I don't want to spend the summer staring at a computer screen, Dad," he said. "I want to get into the golf business. What's the point of working if you don't enjoy what you are doing?"

That stumped me for a second. Then I thought of student loans, bank accounts and the like.

"But if you take the AT&T gig, then you'll get a job that will let you play lots of golf, because you could afford it," I argued (rather feebly, I must admit). "Not many people get this kind of chance."

His reply stopped me in my tracks.

But dad, I don't want to work to enjoy life, I want to enjoy life at work."

There's no answer for that one, particularly since that's exactly what I've been preaching to him for years. Every time he asked me why I was working so many hours, or stressing out about how a story or paper came out, I'd reply that it was because I loved what I was doing. It was, and is, true.

I thought back to all the advice my father and grandfather gave me when I was Alex's age. In retrospect, their advice was good, and I might have been better off if I had taken it. I might be a general in the Army now, or a genetic scientist, if I had.

Instead, I went my own way, followed my own star. I humbly submit that it didn't turn out all that badly.

Part of the reason I made it, despite all my missteps, was the good grounding I received from my father. Even though I might not have followed his suggestions step by step, I did listen and try to understand his reasons for them.

I think Alex has done the same. Sure, I'd love to see him land a six-figure job right out of college (early retirement for Dad?). But I'd much rather think that he can wake up each morning eager to go to work, knowing he's doing something he enjoys.

I guess I'm trying to convince myself that my son is taking my advice, even if he isn't doing what I'd suggest at this moment in time. He has made a good decision.

Can you tell I'm proud?

ABOUT THE LIFE I LEAD

ANOTHER BIG EVENT in my life called for, of course, another column. Getting married late in life does offer a different perspective, to be sure.

Aug. 24, 2000

This getting married after 40 stuff is, to say the least, interesting.

Maria and I have both been married before. We both have kids from previous marriages. Now don't start humming the "Brady Bunch" theme song – the Brady Bunch we are not.

But it does provide some wedding day advantages. It's a ready-made wedding party. We don't have to worry about hurting someone's feelings because they weren't asked to be a bridesmaid or a groomsman. All the slots are filled.

My son Alex is (and always will be) my best man. He'll stand by my side this Saturday, and I bet he won't even drop the ring.

Maria's oldest, Aimee, is her maid of honor. At a touch taller than 6 feet, she could dominate the proceedings – and undoubtedly will take the three-on-three title at the reception.

Our 13-year-old, Charlotte, will be the belle of the ball as the bridesmaid. It's just fortunate there won't be too many 14-year-old boys at the reception – I won't have to keep watch for predators.

Just-turned-11 John is the groomsman and is amazingly handsome in a tux (if we can keep him in it all the way through the ceremony, it will be a miracle). We're trying to convince him to walk his mom down the aisle, but his shyness is putting up an awfully good fight.

That part of an over-40 marriage is, as the kids say, way cool. To have our children share this special day is a dream come true.

There are plenty of other differences, as well. As I was frantically calling motels this week to find rooms for out-of-town family (just talk to me if you think we don't need more hotels in Long Beach), I thought of a few.

For some strange reason, our parents don't seem to feel obligated to pay for the wedding, the rehearsal dinner or the reception. On the other hand, they don't have any interest in planning the thing, either.

Instead of spending weeks dreaming of her big day and going to wedding showers, Maria has been tying pew bows (a big thing, I'm told), going over details and deciding what to do with the aforementioned relatives. Instead of dawdling at bachelor parties and thinking my biggest worry is getting to the chapel on time, I've been trying to pitch in and help with everything from invitations to making sure the photographer shows up.

Speaking of which, handling details such as finding a photographer is the biggest plus of an over-40 wedding. I've been fortunate enough to make many good friends in Long Beach in my time here, and I'm taking full advantage of them all.

The true captain of the ship, Joseph Prevratil, has kindly agreed to perform the ceremony aboard my favorite place in Long Beach, the Queen Mary. The consummate pro behind the camera, John Robinson, is handling the lens. My own personal CD-maniac, Pete Brooks, created a special mix just for the reception. And those are just the ones that come to the forefront of my spinning brain.

By this time next week, it will be all over. But the memories of a special, special day will linger. I wish you could all be there to share it with us – we could use the presents! (Just kidding.)

Instead, I'll just ask for your prayers that this marriage be blessed. I know I already am.

After all, not many old men like me get another chance to get it right – after 40.

ABOUT THE LIFE I LEAD

THE RELATIONSHIP BETWEEN my father and his mother, my grandmother, probably did more to shape my attitude towards family responsibility than anything else in my life. It literally defined the word selfless to me.

I aspire to that standard even today, after both my grandmother and my father have died.

Dec. 28, 2000

Christmas this year has been a particularly intense learning period for me, as well as one unique in my 47 years.

I've already written about the vagaries of joining holiday traditions with a new family. Each holiday day with Maria brings a new surprise.

But the season has brought me more than I expected. We've experienced what is supposed to be a last Christmas for one relative, a definite first Christmas for another and – as of this writing – we've still got more Christmas to come when our kids return from Colorado.

That "last" Christmas probably taught me the most. With one exception, for the last five years, I've been spending Christmas wherever my grandmother was, because it was going to be her last.

She's 91 now, and in very poor health. But, as Uncle John (Dad's brother) has pointed out, she's probably chuckling right now that she got me there for the holiday, and planning on how she'll do it again next year.

That's undoubtedly what has happened in the past. I'd like to think that's what this year is about, too. But somehow I doubt it.

Grandma had some serious emergency surgery this fall – the kind the doctors don't really expect 91-year-olds to survive, much less recover from. She's now dependent on others for virtually everything – something that makes her very angry on the few occasions when she is lucid enough to realize what's going on.

What's most impressive, though, is the care my father and his wife have given her. Dad's no spring chicken at 70, but he has devoted the last several months of his life (and much more, truth be told) to caring for his mother. His wife, Joan, has been right there, doing everything from picking out clothes to helping with bathroom visits.

The Christmas lesson I learned as I watched this ongoing effort was a profound one. It was the true meaning of giving. Father gave knick-knacks for Christmas presents. But for a long time now he has been offering the ultimate gift – his life – for another.

True, it's his mother. There shouldn't be a question about taking care of her or not. Unfortunately, in this modern world of Me-ism, his actions are the exception rather than the rule.

I get a lump in my throat every time I think about his selfless dedication. It is a true example of Christian caring from a man who would never consider himself a Samaritan.

Then there was the first Christmas of our adopted grandson (the only description we can come up with), Erik. The 2-month-old has no clue what all the commotion is about, although I suspect he enjoys all the bright colors and new smells.

When we visited Christmas night, though, I caught myself watching him intently. I saw in him the innocence and purity that is the essence of Christmas.

That babe was, for me, the symbol of the Babe who started it all. He was pure love. He was pure hope. He was the reason to make the world a better place by being the best I could be.

He was Christmas. May we all be as blessed.

ABOUT THE LIFE I LEAD

ONE OF THE real keys to a good column is finding things to write about that other people identify with. There's nothing more universal than mothers, and pretty much nothing more common than a Mother's Day column.

I'd like to think I found a bit of a different approach, pulled from the reality of my life.

May 9, 2002

It's Tuesday morning and I just got off the phone after ordering flowers for Mother's Day. The guy tried to convince me to save 10% by having the flowers delivered early – as in today. I guess that says something about the popularity of flowers for mom, but I passed. What's the point if the flowers are wilted by Mom's Day?

Actually, my mother died more than a decade ago. The flower shops still get my business, though, for Grandma and my dad's wife, Joan.

But I still think of my mom around this time of year. She was less than the perfect mom, if there is such a thing. Her idea of cooking was taking the frozen pizza out of the box. She motivated through guilt and she was a past master of "poor me."

But all of that faded away in the face of her great and abiding love for her children. She was a mother bear in the best sense of the term.

Mom gave me plenty of grief in the privacy of our home, always pushing to "make me a better person." But she was a fierce protector in the mean old world.

I'll never forget the day she charged the umpire when I was thrown out at the plate. I actually was out, but she didn't think so, and she was more than willing to tell the umpire her son never got thrown out.

At the time, I was mortified. This was American Legion baseball, not Little League! Now I think of it and smile.

I've run across tons of mothers in my life, and the good ones all have one thing in common – Mother Bearishness.

The cynical will say that protectiveness is a biological imperative. I say it's love.

I'm less than proud of my multiple marriages, but they have provided me with one great positive – I've gotten to know some great moms. It starts with my own son Alex's mother. She did a great job raising Alex while I tried to support them from a distance (we separated when he was 2 years old).

The results speak for themselves. You're a great mom, Eloise.

Then there is Reetz. Her son, Derek, is graduating from CSULB this month. He's lived with his mom, who was on her own, since he started school here. She's cooked for him, cleaned for him and paid for him to make sure he got through college. The graduation party will be as much for Reetz as it is for Derek.

The results speak for themselves. You're a great mom, Reetz.

Now there's Maria. Her children are her reason for living. I only hope that Aimee, Charlotte and John can come to appreciate that sooner rather than later (they're still kids, after all).

Maria's "mom heart" is so big that she brings in strays. Our psuedo-grandson, Erik, is just the latest in a long line to benefit from Mama Bear Maria.

The results speak for themselves. You're a great mom, Maria.

Those are just the great moms I've been privileged to know closely. I know there are many others.

As a mere man, I would be lying if I claimed to understand that mother love. But I do know I'm awfully glad it's there. Mothers are God's gift to us all.

The results speak for themselves. You're a great mom, all you moms. Have a special Mother's Day.

ABOUT THE LIFE I LEAD

MY GRANDFATHER ON my father's side died from emphysema, a two-pack a day man. My mother died in her early 50s of a heart attack, obese, and nearly three packs a day.

Still, I was a Marlboro man. When I tried to quit, which was often, I was able to wear the patch, chew the gum and still crave – and smoke – a cigarette. Until one day in 2002.

Aug. 29, 2002

Big health news from the Saltzgaver front – I've quit smoking!

In a weak New Year's Resolution moment some eight months ago, I promised to give up the noxious weed by the end of 2002. I've managed it a whole four months early.

That may not be a big deal to some, but it is to me. After all, I've been smoking for 30 years, and I've used everything from the patch to subliminal messages to try to quit.

But on Aug. 19, I quit for good. Just like that. I'll tell you how I did it, but I plead with you to not try the same approach.

I had a heart attack.

You read right. At 48 years old, I found myself doing that clutch my chest, gasp for breath thing.

I should have been scared, I suppose, but it simply hurt too much for that. The scared came later. At the time, I just wanted the pain to stop.

Maria, who wakes up if I move my big toe, was dressed before I was. She drove me to the Memorial Medical Center emergency room and I stumbled in under my own power while she parked the car.

She says I looked like Quasimodo as I walked into the hospital. It worked – I was being treated less than a minute later.

This was at 1:45 a.m. By 3:30, they were taking me up to the cath lab, where they routinely perform miracles. (A side trip into the maternity ward provided a little comic relief.) I was on a cold slab, surrounded by high-tech marvels, by 3:45.

Dr. E. Vanneta, who I later learned is one of the best around, looked at my heart by sticking a tube through my groin and up an artery, cleaned out a blockage in said artery and implanted a stent (think PVC pipe repair) in the same place. I was on my way to the recovery room by 4:45.

I've been writing about the heart programs at Memorial for years, often mentioning the fact they are among the top in the nation. But nothing beats personal experience. These guys are good. All that time spent on Gazette Newspapers' "Hearts For Long Beach" charity looks well-spent now.

The good doctor later told me the heart attack likely was caused by a clot in a narrow artery, probably caused by smoking. Go figure.

The outpouring of calls, cards and flowers was touching and appreciated. Many stepped up, and continue to step up, to help around our house (which is, of course, in the midst of yet another home improvement project). Most importantly, my guys and gals here at the Gazette reached down and turned out some great papers without me (darn, and I thought I was indispensable).

Thank you to all who have expressed their concern. I hope you will forgive me for not naming names – those drugs the first day or two didn't do much for my concentration.

Call it a miracle of modern medicine or the grace of God, but I was out of the hospital on Wednesday. I drove myself to the pharmacy that afternoon for the fist-full of drugs I now must take every day. I've gone to several events - Editor Kurt Helin's wedding top among them – and as you can see, I'm doing a bit of work just a week after the attack.

But I'm not smoking. And I'm watching what I eat (if you have Jack In The Box stock, sell!). Once I get my strength back, I might even (gasp) start an exercise program.

I thanked God for each day before Aug. 19, but there's a little added fervor in that prayer now. I suspect there will be more changes in my life due to this brush with mortality. But this one is a pretty good start.

I don't smoke anymore. That's a good thing.

THE JUXTAPOSITION OF young versus old is always worth exploring. When you add a personal connection, it becomes engaging. When you touch on the beginning of an adult life with the end of an old life, it becomes compelling.

It certainly was to me.

May 29, 2003

Ying versus yang. Young versus old. The best of times versus the worst of times.

I do my very best not to look at things as black or white, to the frequent consternation of my pastor and some of our more literal-minded readers. Situations are virtually never all one way or another.

But I sure felt like I got a look at the ends of the spectrum this past weekend.

Let's start with the good. For the second straight year, my son Alex came out from Colorado so he and I could take a little Memorial Day weekend golf trip. He flew in here, and we drove to St. George, Utah, a golf mecca where my father has retired.

Alex is 24 years old. He's just two years removed from college. He is buying his own home, and spends his weekends fly fishing, skiing or golfing. He's ready for a significant relationship, but he's not so desperate that he's chasing girls every Friday and Saturday night.

In short, he's got pretty much his whole life in front of him, and he's got it together. He's doing good things and enjoying himself at the same time.

On the other end of the spectrum is my grandmother, Dorine Saltzgaver. She'll be 94 years old in July – if she lives that long. She also lives in St. George, at an assisted-care center.

Grandma has lived a full life. She has been the stalwart of the family. She was always dignified, wise and with a sparkle in her eye.

Which is why it seems so unfair that she is such a shell of a woman now. Emergency surgeries under anesthesia and simple old age has taken away the woman who beat me at golf when she was 80 with the adage 100 yards straight gets you there faster than 200 yards crooked.

"It's sad," Alex said after we had visited. "She was such a strong woman. It's hard to understand."

What he was talking about is why, after such a vibrant, fulfilling life, Grandma has to suffer now. I'm ashamed to say we couldn't spend more than 10 minutes with her – it was too painful for us, not her. For the last two years, this woman who once took care of the entire family has been unable to do more than sit and sleep.

The phrase skin and bones doesn't adequately describe what this once-statuesque woman has become. Her wheelchair seemed to swallow her.

In the short time we were there, she faded away twice. She simply didn't have the energy to keep her eyes open.

"I'm so tired, always tired," she whispered as Alex and I kissed her goodbye.

We were quiet as we drove away. There seemed little we could say. I told Alex that I simply couldn't imagine how my father manages to deal with it every day, and still maintain his love of life. But he does.

An hour later, we were on a golf course, under a brilliant blue sky. The 24-year-old wound up and hit a drive that bounced up the fairway some 340 yards away. Straight as a string. He turned to me and grinned.

"Boy, this is fun," he said.

He was right. It was. And somehow, in a way I don't think I can explain, the whole ying and yang of it all made a little more sense.

That's life.

MY GRANDMOTHER SALTZGAVER was, and remains, a person who I aspired to be like. Her calm competence always impressed me, and her ability to enjoy life was enviable.

Then there was the love. Saying goodbye was hard. But I hit it straight, and kept on walking.

Aug. 21, 2003

The last time I wrote about my grandmother was the week after Memorial Day.

I wrote bemoaning the fact that she was suffering through her last days of life. No more. Her suffering is over.

Dorine Saltzgaver died on Aug. 12, 2003, at the age of 94. She died in her sleep, passing peacefully.

After visiting her on Memorial Day, I worried that I wouldn't be able to shake the image of her then. She was shriveled, unhappy and uncertain why she was still alive. Physical maladies had left her unable to do more than eat and sleep.

I'm pleased to report that her death has been a blessing, both for her and for me. She suffers no more. And I am now free to remember her as she truly was – a wise, happy woman who taught me what it was to live a decent life.

Many memories are swirling in my mind, from visiting Grandma at her house in Bond, Colo., in my youngest days to bringing my son Alex to her to show him off – and get her blessing. But two short anecdotes sum up what I think my grandmother was all about.

The first doesn't even involve me. It was related to me by Alex.

Five or six years ago, Alex was traveling out to visit me and stopped in St. George, Utah, to say hello to Grandma. By that time, various physical ailments had caused her to move into an assisted care center with other seniors. She was, after all, 87 or 88 years old.

"We knocked on her door, but she wasn't there," Alex said.

"Some lady said she might be working at the gift shop, because she did that a lot. But she wasn't there either.

"We checked at the front desk, but she hadn't gone out. We were about ready to give up and were walking out when we went by the recreation room and heard her laughing. We walked in and she was playing pool with some old guy. She said she was teaching him the game."

Alex still tells that story. But my defining moment with Grandma goes further back. She was 79 or 80, still living alone in Lake Havasu City, Ariz.

I came for a visit and she convinced me to go play nine holes of golf with her — she was a member of a club there. This was when I still fancied myself an athlete but before I had seriously started playing golf.

I lugged my bag of 15 clubs to the first tee and looked around, waiting for her to come out of the starter's shack. She walked up, a seven wood (really made of wood, I might add) in her hand. When I asked if I could get the rest of her clubs, she just smiled and said, "This is all I need."

She hit her first drive about 100 yards down the fairway. I smiled indulgently and promptly ripped a 250-yard drive. Unfortunately, it was about 20 yards to the left of the fairway, in the Arizona desert.

I hacked my way to an 8 on that first hole. She used the seven wood to make a 3-foot putt for a 5.

To make a long story short, Grandma beat me soundly that day. She never hit a ball more than 100 yards, but she never hit one out of the fairway, either. She didn't pontificate on her philosophy of golf, or life. She just played the game and smiled.

She just hit them straight, and kept walking.

That's how I'll remember her. Thank you for being in my life, Grandma. God bless.

TRYING TO EXPLAIN how "real life" gets in the way of reporting when you're running a tiny operation always includes a danger that readers will think you're whining. That's even more the case when you feel like whining. I tried to combat that danger with humor. Hopefully, it was successful more often than not.

April 22, 2004

One of these days, I'll stop thinking I'm Tim "the Toolman" Taylor. Unfortunately, last weekend wasn't one of those days. I decided (with some serious help from my wife, Maria) that it was time to replace our 60-year-old bathroom sink with a new vanity and all the accoutrements.

For those of you who just emerged from winter hibernation, last weekend was the Toyota Grand Prix of Long Beach. I spend most of Saturday and Sunday working the races, taking pictures.

So what does that have to do with installing a sink? Well, anyone in his right mind wouldn't have started such a project without having an open weekend. But my ego got the better of me, and I was sure I could put it together in the hour or two between photo assignments.

I had, after all, bought the completely assembled vanity cabinet, the one-piece sink and the "easy to install" faucet kit. And plumbing is in my genes – my dearly departed grandfather was a master plumber, fixing pipes to finance his love of training quarter horses.

Things started out well Saturday. We got home after the wet Pro/Celebrity race and I had successfully removed the old sink in less than an hour. About half that time was spent trying to get the rusted screws to move so I could take the bracket off the wall. But no blood was spilled.

Then I tried to slip the fully assembled cabinet up against the wall. Apparently, the assemblers forgot that water pipes have a tendency to run up walls in old bathrooms. Still, the portable jigsaw created the three notches quickly, and I was moving forward.

The faucet attached to the sink easily enough. But the vanity was two inches taller than the old sink, which made the drain two inches short.

Deal with that later. I had about 45 minutes before I had to leave to shoot the Miss Toyota pageant (the most important assignment of the weekend). I turned my attention to connecting the water.

I grabbed one of the "flexible" connector pipes – it broke in my hand. That was it. No sink for Saturday night. I'd have to get new connectors and install them on Sunday, after the race.

Fast forward to the hardware store after Tracy's victory Sunday. None of the hardware looks familiar (none of it is 60 years old). I get all the stuff I think I need to cobble the connections together.

At home, I spend 45 minutes trying to turn the water off at the water meter. Two skinned knuckles later, I remember the valve next to the house. Turns out it doesn't just turn off the water to the sprinkler system, like I thought.

Take the old connectors off. (That's after two trips to the tool store trying to get an open-end wrench of the right size. I settled for a second crescent wrench.) Discover I bought female connectors when I needed males (go figure).

Back to the hardware store – a different one, since I'm too embarrassed to go back to the last one. Buy the opposite of what I bought before.

I get everything together once and have Maria stand in front of the sink while I go out in the dark (it's dark around 8 p.m. these days) to turn on the water. She screams. I go back and put one of the connectors back on while she cleans up the water that came shooting out.

In sum, it took about eight hours to do a one-hour job. I have skinned knuckles and my head looks like I used it for a battering ram (which, if the cabinet could talk, might turn out to be true).

But we have a new sink and vanity, and I did it myself. Let's just keep the struggles between us, okay?

After all, I'm angling for a show called Harry the Handyman.

IT NEVER CEASES to amaze me how something simple invariably turned complicated when I tried to do it myself. But I could always count on the job to provide column fodder. The shade is still in place, by the way.

Feb. 6, 2006

It was supposed to be a simple project.

I've replaced a number of light fixtures in my day. Most of the rooms in my vintage house have ceiling fans (no air conditioning) because I put them there.

So I didn't even flinch when Maria spotted a hand-painted ceramic ceiling shade during our recent trip to Mexico. "It will be perfect in the kitchen," she exclaimed (really, she exclaims when she sees stuff like this). I figured it would take 45 minutes, an hour tops.

So last Friday, I dismantled the industrial-strength fixture I had put in the kitchen just last year. Then I stood there, Mexican shade in hand, trying to figure out how to attach the thing to the ceiling.

Remember that this work of art came from central Mexico, not central Home Depot. There were no little pre-drilled screw holes, no nifty attachment plate.

There was a central stem with two wires sticking out. So I decided to use the old fixture ceiling plate, putting the work of art against that.

The ceiling plate has those swell little slots where you slide it over two screws, turn slightly and you're done. That might have worked, except the ceramic art covered up the slots.

After holding the contraption, which weighed a good 10 pounds, up to the ceiling for 10 minutes trying to connect slots and screws by feel, I gave that one up.

The ceiling plate was larger than the shade, though, so I figured I could drill holes outside of the shade and attach the plate that way. Good idea, except the wires had to be connected before the drilling took place.

After holding the assembly up for another 15 minutes, I managed to drill one hole. I missed the stud, and the drywall ceiling clearly wasn't going to support the ceramic.

Three hours gone, and it's starting to get dark. I had to get some light back in the kitchen to cook dinner.

So the ceiling plate went back where it originally was, and the ceramic shade became a hanging lamp, holding on by the wire – literally.

Saturday, I took the whole thing apart again and crawled all the way across the attic to get at it from above. I was going to take the power box cover off and attach the ceramic shade directly to the bracket.

The mummified fruit rat next to the fixture was a nifty addition to the adventure. After considering its demise, I realized that the bracket I was counting on was attached directly to the cover.

I finally managed to get the thing up with plenty of extra wire and a few Boy Scout knots. It should be good until the next earthquake. I left the mummified rat up there for good luck.

My reward? "It looks great," Maria said. "Now if you can just patch those holes around it and touch up the paint a little."

20 YEARS OF SALT

SOME OF THE best reader response I received has been from my retelling of attempts at home improvement projects. I rarely had to exaggerate the faux pas to start the humor, and I have little problem with self-deprecating comments, at least in print.

The kitchen upgrade was a biggie. And I only had to call someone to redo the floor.

June 29, 2006

The challenge has been issued.

I've trained for this moment. I have my plans, the materials have arrived, the vacation time applied for and approved.

I'm redoing the kitchen.

That faithful reader up in Belmont Heights knows what this means — an adventure worthy of Indiana Jones playing the part of Tim "The Toolman" Taylor. For the rest of you, let me give you a clue of what's in store — my wife, Maria, is spending the next five weeks in Colorado.

I'm really not sure what all the fuss is about. I've successfully redone our bathroom sink with just one week and eight trips to the hardware store. I rewired part of the attic and there's only one patch where I stepped through the ceiling (I managed to put that in a closet, too).

Past projects have been family affairs. Maria helped when I put in ceiling fans, and her hair grew back in just fine. We assembled the grill together, and it only took me cooking a half-dozen meals and she was talking to me again.

It only took a month when we decided to rip up the wall-to-wall carpet and refinish the gorgeous hardwood floors. Of course, it would have been done sooner if I hadn't had that heart attack.

I was able to put new wall cabinets in the kitchen a couple of years ago. My shoulder is just about back to normal now, although my golf partners still have a tendency to laugh at my swing.

So why did Maria schedule family reunions four states away this summer?

Well, I will admit this little project could get interesting. My 1940s house came complete with built-in cabinets, and I mean built in. Some master craftsman created these things board by board, attaching everything together.

Then there is the tile work. These are real tiles, attached to a chicken wire/cement base. Mess up just a little bit taking it out and I'll be drywalling on top of everything else.

Plans call for a new sink and a built-in dishwasher – the new sink has two drains where the old one has one, and the current dishwasher hooks up to the kitchen faucet for its water.

Forget about making sure the cabinet doors close and the drawers move in and out. We're talking about replumbing the kitchen to accommodate the sink and dishwasher, and wiring under the counter to power the thing.

As Maria left, she warned that water and electricity don't mix. Well, we'll just see about that, won't we?

If I actually manage to complete the cabinets, countertop, sink and dishwasher, I will redo the kitchen floor. My experts tell me I don't have to take up the 60-year-old linoleum to put down new tile. But they haven't explained how I get rid of those roller-coaster bumps in the old stuff.

When I planned this little home improvement project, I put in for one week of vacation, and I'm taking that now. Is a second week required before the end of summer? Of course not. But just in case . Hey, Dave, can you write a few headlines come late July?

"A PINCH OF Salt" has been many things over the years, but it has always been one thing – a statement of philosophy. That philosophy has been influenced, bent and reshaped by forces and people in my life.

And, as is the case with this column, the writing of A Pinch often helped crystallize it, at least at that time.

Nov. 23, 2006

Have you happened to catch the "This I Believe" series that's been running for the last year or so on National Public Radio?

It, like so many other things in the media today, actually is a reprise of an old idea – in this case Edward R. Murrow's old radio series where he asked prominent people to explain guiding principles in their lives.

The modern version expands the idea to let "everyday folk" have a chance to explore their core values.

I have been eternally blessed with a weekly opportunity to give my own "This I Believe." In this week of bringing to the fore the many things we all have to be thankful for, I have to say I am very thankful for this column – and, of course, the kind people who read it.

Admittedly, there have been plenty of times when I've been flippant in this space. I've gone for the laugh as often as I've gone for the deeper meaning.

I've used it to blow off steam (remember when the car burglars stole my camera, but not my golf clubs?) and I've used it to express my personal grief (I still try to "hit 'em straight and keep on walking," grandma). I've used it to brag about my family, my pets, even my church.

Some people say I've shared too much of my personal life, and perhaps I have. Laying your spiritual life out for all to criticize might not be such a good idea. Trials and travails at home can be uncomfortable to talk about.

I inevitably seem to err on the side of sharing.

I've tried to give a pinch or two to our community leaders, and to those who would lead our community whether we like it or not. I've taken up causes I believe in.

But, serious or light, personal or political, I tell you what I believe here. The goal was and is to put a bit of a human face on this paper.

It has worked. I've lost count of the times people have come up and said, "you don't know me, but I know you." Then they proceed to prove it.

I'm thankful for that. I'm thankful for those who disagree with me, and let me know it. I'm thankful for those I've managed to touch.

I'm thankful for the opportunity to spark thought and debate. I consider that opportunity a responsibility, and hope I discharge that responsibility at least adequately.

Together, we can make a difference, and I hope this column continues to be a conduit to help that happen. It can if we, if I, let it.

I'm thankful for you, gentle reader.

After all, if a column falls in the woods and there is no one to read it, I don't think it makes a sound.

This, I believe.

WATCHING SOMEONE DIE is a hard thing. Watching someone you know die is a very hard thing. Knowing that the person dying is important to someone you love, and sitting with that person, is very, very hard.

It is also one of the most important things I've done.

Jan. 11, 2007

Technology in 2007 is an amazing thing.

I'm sitting in St. George, Utah, as I write this column for Long Beach, Calif. Once it is done, I can push a button and send it to a computer in Gazette Central. No phone wires, modems or anything.

Amazing.

I'm sitting in a facility called the Dixie Regional Medical Center. I'm looking at a hospital bed that clearly could fly given the proper pilot. No wonder it takes so long to get through medical school – it would take me a good year just to learn how to operate a modern bed.

Actually, I haven't seen too many doctors. This intensive care unit is staffed by nurses – a lot of highly efficient, clearly caring and obviously well-trained nurses. Outside the door, there's a sign of the times – notice that there are five full-time day shift positions available. But that's a different story for a different time.

St. George has a state-of-the-art medical facility thanks in large part to the Mormon church. That would be the Church of Latter Day Saints. These folks have money, and aren't afraid to spend it. The ICU room I am in has to hold $250,000 in equipment, is larger than my bedroom at home, and is one of 17 in the facility.

All around me, technological medical miracles are taking place. One man just returned from triple bypass surgery. People who would have been given no shot of survival just years ago are living for years.

The woman on the bed I'm looking at is still alive because of the technology. She couldn't breathe when Dad brought her in.

The doctor suggested trying a ventilator for a couple of days — not as life support, but to open up lungs squashed by a disease kin to emphysema, and to give Joan a chance to recover some strength. She'd worn herself out just trying to get a breath.

After more than three days, it was time to see if Joan could make it on her own. After all, she had a living will, and the doctor had said this bit of technology was therapy, not life support.

Only it didn't work. Joan refused to wake up, even though she had been taken off the sedation.

Another new technology was brought in to give her body a last chance. The new gadget didn't breathe for her, but forced oxygen into her lungs every time she did breathe.

Twenty-four hours later, technology had failed. If anything, she was worse. Dad and Joan's daughter, Judy, made the tough decision, and technology was taken away. A little morphine was added in the hope her last hours could be made comfortable.

Only Joan, or Joan's keeper, wasn't ready to let go. Four hours after the life support was turned off, Joan was better.

It wouldn't last. Six hours later, the call came to come back because she was failing.

Joan still wasn't ready. She made it through the night. The doctor came by in the morning. His demeanor said clearly, it wasn't a matter of whether, but when. But neither the technology nor the doctor would be able to say when.

"Sometimes we doctors think we are in control, but we aren't, really," the wise man, whom I sadly can't identify, said. "That's up to someone else."

Twelve hours later, either Joan hasn't given up or the one in charge isn't quite done with what he's teaching. Joan's in a Cessna bed now instead of the Lear Jet, letting someone else have a chance with our wondrous technology. Maybe it will be the one in charge's will that they make it.

God's will be done.

Epilogue: Joan Saltzgaver died at 9:30 a.m. Jan. 9, 48 hours after being taken off life support.

ABOUT THE LIFE I LEAD

ONE OF THE drawbacks of a personal column is a tendency to write about personal milestones. It also is one of the best ways to let your readers know who you are. There's no doubt I wrote this for Maria. But I believe I also wrote it for all those other women, and men, who found themselves back in school with students the age of their children.

May 24, 2007

By this time next week, Maria Saltzgaver will be a college graduate.

This is a big deal. I know that she is only one of more than 6,000 students receiving a degree from California State University, Long Beach, but she's special. And not just because of her last name, either.

Maria is among those ubiquitously labeled "returning students." She actually got an AA (Associate of Arts) degree a long time ago from a community college in Colorado, but then ventured into the real world, raising three children and working.

When the corporate merger/downsizing game so popular in the publishing world caught Maria in its vortex some six years ago, she decided to go back to school. She reasoned that more and current skills would make her more valuable in the job market. I couldn't disagree.

But you need to know a bit about Maria to understand just how brave this decision showed her to be. She was a shy woman, willing to stay in the background. Her priority then (and now) is her children. Middle daughter and youngest son were just entering middle school.

Still, she started stepping out shortly after she started classes at Long Beach City College. She joined the honors program. She found out what it would take to transfer seamlessly to CSULB, and she added classes to make sure she was truly prepared – not just on paper, but with her knowledge.

By the time she started at The Beach, son John was in high school. I won't go into detail, but let's just say that John and his education have been of the high-maintenance variety.

The shy young blonde I married blossomed in the Beach sand. She joined more honors classes and became very involved in the business mentoring program.

Her real coming-out party took place a couple of weeks ago, at the mentoring program awards dinner. I watched proudly as my (former) wallflower "worked the room" with confidence and style. She deserved it when she was given the night's big prize, the Leadership In Action Award.

Maria has worked incredibly hard for something she wanted intensely – a Bachelor of Science degree from CSULB's school of business. She valued the chance to get an education, and made the most of it by doing what it took.

I don't care what you say, it is harder for a mature adult to survive the rigors of college life than it is for the teens and 20-somethings that make up the vast majority of the CSULB student body. I could only shake my head as I watched Maria do the all-nighters and pound out the papers I had struggled with 30 years ago.

It is said that pride is one of the seven deadly sins. Well, when she walks the stage next Wednesday to accept that diploma, I'm afraid I'll be the one sinning.

Okay, it does have something to do with the last name. But it also has something to do with watching someone I care for achieve a lofty and hard-to-reach goal.

Congratulations, dear. It's your day. You did it. Hooray.

ABOUT THE LIFE I LEAD

I WAS ONE of John's biggest challenges. I was the stepfather he didn't want.

There's no doubt he was one of my biggest challenges, too. I don't think I ever figured out what might work. But somehow it worked out. This decision of his was a key.

Aug. 2, 2007

Have you ever felt like you would jinx something good if you dared to talk about it?

You know what I mean – that job interview went really well and, even though they haven't offered the job yet, you just know they're going to give it to you (as long as you don't tell anyone you might get it).

Or you're certain you've aced the test even though you don't have the grade back yet, but you refuse to look at the book to see if you really got the question right.

That's where I'm at right now with my stepson, John. His high school career has been a struggle, to be charitable. He thinks he invented teen-aged angst, and sometimes I believe him.

It didn't seem to matter what I or his mother tried, John was going to do it his way – the hard way. Watching that was painful.

Did I mention that being a step-dad is tough? I've been disappointed with my performance.

But something has changed. John turned it all around about a month ago. I have no idea what happened.

He actually did the work required to pass his summer school class – the same one he refused to even attend his senior year – and now is a signature away from his high school diploma.

He certainly didn't become Wally Cleaver at home, but he did turn into a responsive human being. We actually had some civil, if short, conversation.

For the last six months, he has claimed he was joining the Marines when he got out of school. He's claimed many things in the last few years, and pretty much none have come true.

But he's making this come true. He has followed through with all the necessary commitments, and is just more than a week away from shipping out to boot camp.

So why would I take the chance of jinxing what I believe to be a very positive end to a very tough, even negative, road?

Because I need to tell John I'm proud of him.

I'm proud that he came to realize that he had to work to get something he valued. I'm proud that he came to realize his mother wasn't picking on him, but was loving him.

I'm proud that he wants to serve his country. I'm proud that he is becoming a man.

I fear that if I were to tell him those things face-to-face, he would feel compelled to prove me wrong somehow. As perverse as that might sound, I've done it myself and know it's possible to do such a thing, even when you know you are only hurting yourself.

So instead of telling him privately, I'm telling the entire world – or at least that small portion that includes those who read "A Pinch." I guess I'm hoping he gets the message by osmosis or something.

Think of it as an end-around. I'm fooling the team of jinx here.

You can help. If you happen to see a tall, gangly kid with a blonde buzz cut, tell him, "Harry said he's proud of you."

The jinx will never know. In fact, I think I'll tempt fate one more time.

God bless you, John. You're doing good.

ABOUT THE LIFE I LEAD

THE DEATH OF a parent is one of the most traumatic things to happen in our lives – not just my feeling, but proven over and over again. When it happened to me, there was no way to do anything but share it. That sharing made it – not easy, but easier.

April 22, 2009

I've spent the last week watching the world through the open door of a hospital room.

For a change, I wasn't the one in the bed. I wish I had been. But more of that later.

What I found fascinating was what I saw outside of that door – and how those outside reacted to what was inside.

For the most part, people were absorbed in their own concerns. No surprise there. Hospitals, especially oncology floors, are places of great concern.

Some passersby were clearly there to visit patients. Most stared straight ahead, or checked room numbers as they walked by.

You could tell how their loved ones were doing by the expression on their faces. Some were concerned, others resigned. Some were hopeful, others happy.

You knew which patients were going home by watching their visitors.

There were a few – very few – who managed to get beyond their own concerns. These were the folks who looked into the hospital room door.

Some looked with frank curiosity; they likely looked at all of life that way. Others had a look of dread, imposing their current experience on me.

Then there were those who made eye contact. Without exception, those eyes held sympathy. I hope I conveyed the same message in return.

Of course there were plenty of nurses, nurses' assistants and doctors. I was impressed with the almost unanimous air of professionalism leavened with care for the people they touched. They eased pain, and made things better where they could.

These people managed to do difficult jobs while showing that they valued the individuals they were dealing with. How so many managed to have the strength to do that day after day is beyond me.

I guess what I'm trying to say is that I've seen a lot of caring, concerned people over the last week. And I've come to the conclusion that they were caring about the right things.

As compared to what? Well, I know that I get awfully wrapped up in the day-to-day concerns of our fair city, and the petty fights among factions here. It is my job, after all, and I do think it's important.

But when we allow our worlds to revolve around those things, it might not be using the best set of priorities.

I know the man who was lying in that bed would have told me that. His watchwords were service to others, caring for the family and doing the right thing – always in sacrifice to his own concerns.

It's what he taught me, and what I've recommitted myself to do. It's the best way I know how to honor the memory of my father.

Harry Mack Saltzgaver III died on the afternoon of Sunday, April 19, 2009, in St. George, Utah. He's in a better place now. God bless you, Dad. And thank you. For everything.

ABOUT THE LIFE I LEAD

I WAS A Colorado boy. Christmas meant a white Christmas, not just Bing singing "White Christmas." Adjusting to a Southern California holiday season remains a fascination to me, even today. It certainly has its charms.

Dec. 9, 2009

Why do we have this fascination with holiday decorations?

I spent much of a cold Sunday this week in my front yard, hanging, adjusting and readjusting Christmas lights. I'm fairly certain I wasn't the only Clark Griswold in Long Beach, either.

I have a theory about December decorations. I believe we as a society need to do it to make ourselves feel good. It has added punch in the northern hemisphere as it is the beginning of winter and we need something to smile about.

That's certainly the case this year, isn't it? I think that might be why we saw a record crowd at the Belmont Shore Christmas Parade despite low (at least Southern California low) temperatures and a later than ever start time. It was a feel-good experience, and it was free.

Back to the decorating.

Maria loves Disneyland, and we go there frequently, particularly around the holidays. They do some pretty amazing things to the Enchanted Castle, Haunted Mansion and It's A Small World.

But the real over-the-top is how they decorate the trees. There has to be more lights in one of their trees than there are in my whole block. It would take me a month just to string all the lights in a single Disney tree.

Yet that is the standard we strive to attain.

It starts with getting the supplies. We've been accumulating decorations for a decade or so. That should be a good thing, but the fact is, Christmas decorations come with a guaranteed planned obsolescence. That's particularly true of outdoor lights.

Last year, we spent hours trying to find the bulbs that were causing the strings to stay stubbornly dark. Then we put them up, and some immediately went dark again. The sense of frustration easily outweighed the feel-good we were supposed to be getting.

So we decided to convert to LED this year. Big energy savings were promised, along with higher reliability and longer life.

The drawback (there's always drawback) was cost. LED decorations are new and hot, and the price the stores are getting reflects that. So we couldn't convert in one fell swoop. At least we couldn't if there was going to be sufficient holiday cheer in Maria's eyes.

Of course, while we were buying lights, we had to look at some other decorations as well. We got a few things. Then it came back to the tree.

You see, a big part of the Disney tree is the profusion of large lighted balls. The multi-colored balls emulate Christmas tree ornaments even though they are in deciduous trees.

Flash forward (or back, depending on your perspective) and you'll see me staring at the mighty Sycamore that stands in my front yard. The first time it branches is a good 12 feet off the ground.

I have four glow globes, about 8 inches in diameter, by my side. Maria points. "I think a couple there, and a couple there on that second branch."

Ever obedient, I stretch the 16-foot extension ladder past its recommended height until the top touches the trunk 20 feet above the ground. Globe in one hand, heavy-duty stapler in the back pocket, I climb. And climb. And climb.

I can tell you categorically that there is no way to staple a large decoration's hanger to a tree one-handed. Have you ever hung on to a ladder by your knees? Cirque du Soleil performers have nothing on me.

Then those dreaded words came. I knew they would. "I think it would look better a few inches that way." I leaned a little further.

Long story semi-short, the job got done, at least until this weekend. I think I saw another string of lights out for checking and eventual placement.

Still, I have to admit that when I drove up to my decorated house Monday night, I smiled. That's what it is all about, isn't it?

I TRIED TO share all of the important moments of my life in "A Pinch," and this was indeed important to me. Publishing a book is the ultimate goal for most writers, and this book was a labor of love. There's too much hubris here, but I tried to temper it with a little humor.

June 23, 2010

Have you ever avoided talking about something to avoid jinxing it?

You know what I mean – when you're on the verge of buying a house, you don't talk about the house you want until the contract is signed. Or you interview for a job, but you haven't heard back yet.

I first discovered this rule of silence while playing baseball. You never talk to a pitcher in the middle of throwing a no-hitter. Hitting streak? Keep your mouth shut.

Well, for the last three years, I've studiously avoided telling anyone what I was doing on Friday afternoons, lots of weekends and occasional late nights. No, it wasn't illegal, or even immoral (at least I don't think it was).

I was trying to write a book.

It's something virtually anyone who writes dreams of doing. Get a bunch of newspaper reporters together, and at least half will tell you that writing a book is one of their life goals.

But I wasn't anxious to talk about it. I didn't want to jinx the project, but I think I also was more than a little afraid that I wouldn't complete it. The pressure was less if I didn't tell anybody what I was trying to do (which also is why I didn't tell anyone when I quit smoking, or when I start dieting).

I was committed to finishing pretty much from the beginning, though. You don't waste hours of important people's time, then not have anything to show.

For a good year, I interviewed Beverly O'Neill almost every Friday afternoon. I had been very careful to wait until she had left office to even approach her about the idea, and it took forever to convince her, but she finally said yes.

She was gracious with her time, and only reluctant when talking about her triumphs. It took some time, but eventually she was willing to talk about her hard times and the rare failure.

Then I talked with her friends, employees and colleagues. I read everything I could find about her, from doctoral dissertations and books to profiles in rival newspapers.

I still didn't tell anyone outside the process what was going on. To tell the truth, I was leery about even telling the people I was interviewing. And I sure didn't tell them when I thought it would be done.

But it did get done. After another six months of editing – which primarily involved convincing Beverly to leave some of the nice stuff about her in – the manuscript was set to submit.

I called it "Passionately Positive: The Beverly O'Neill Story." It was short – some said too short. I said it was in newspaper style, or rather, my style: Concise and hopefully to the point.

I found a way to get the thing published. The publisher said I needed to identify the target audience, and a subtitle might help do that.

That might have been the best piece of advice I received during this whole process. It is subtitled, "Leadership Through Inspiration." It defines, in my opinion, Beverly's life.

But back to the whole don't jinx it thing. I still refused to talk about the book, waiting until I actually had a copy in my hand.

Even then, I waited. I wanted to have it in the bookstores, or at least know when they were going to be there, before I did a story in the Gazette.

I underestimated the power of Beverly O'Neill's legacy.

A few invitations were sent out for a quiet book-launching event. Okay, there were more than a few, but then, marketer Dianne Ripley always did think big. And a few of those invites landed in the hands of other publications and Web sites.

Turns out, a biography about Beverly O'Neill is news. At least it was news to some, as Web sites and even the Press-Telegram saw fit to give it some ink (what do you call that on the Internet – bandwidth?).

They had scooped me. On my own book.

Well, at least I hadn't jinxed it. Or I don't think I did.

The book will be in general release early in July, with copies in Long Beach bookstores. You can also go to the Amazon or Barnes & Noble sites or to www.outskirtspress.com/passionatelypositive to order a copy.

Let me know what you think. Did I jinx it?

ABOUT THE LIFE I LEAD

I RARELY USED my column to write about the paper, especially if it involved a particular instance. I certainly believe in owning up, it's just that the correction typically is the proper place for that.

But I made a lot of people unhappy with this one, so I made the exception.

Sept. 15, 2010

Most of the time, actually about 95% of the time, I love my job.

That other 5% is usually right after I've discovered that I've made a mistake. Or, if you like, we'll expand that to the royal We.

When there's something wrong in the paper, I feel physical pain. I'm the executive editor, so whenever there's a mistake, it is ultimately my fault.

It's hard to describe the feeling when I've personally generated the mistake. And when the mistake is something I know better than, it can be downright debilitating.

I made such a mistake last week.

To the entire membership of the Long Beach Assistance League, present, past and future, I offer my most sincere and humble apology.

In last week's edition, I wrote an editorial (I don't think it's a big secret that I write the editorials above this column after consulting the esteemed editorial board) praising, or attempting to praise, all the various folks who help enhance education in Long Beach. When planning the editorial, I told myself to be sure to include two fine female philanthropic organizations – the Assistance League and the Junior League.

But when I wrote the piece, I inexplicably left out the Assistance League. Worse, I gave credit to the Junior League for Operation School Bell, the signature program of the Rick Rackers, an Assistance League auxiliary.

It wasn't a Freudian slip or anything like that – it was just a mistake. An inexcusable mistake, because I've personally been involved with the Assistance League and the Junior League for a number of years.

We've done stories on Operation School Bell, I've been to the Assistance League's impressive home on Spring Street a number of times, etc.

But there it was in print – Operation School Bell with no Assistance League.

Truth be told, I discovered the error Thursday morning, before the first phone call (the first, but far from the last). I always look at the paper when it arrives from the printer, and the error seemed to jump off the page at me. Errors have a way of doing that.

I fixed the mistake immediately on our Web site, www.gazettes.com, and fixed the editorial before it ran in the Downtown and Uptown Gazettes on Friday (which is why some of you won't have a clue of what I'm talking about). But the damage was done.

It was in print. That, gentle reader, is both the boon and the bane of my profession.

When I, or we, do something right such as offer a profound insight or a clever turn of phrase, it not only has our name on it, it is preserved for posterity (if only on the bottom of the birdcage). You thought newspapers kept back issues so things could be looked up, didn't you? Think again. They are there to feed battered egos in time of need.

What can a newspaper guy do to fix a mistake once the paper has gone to press, though? Should I run around with a huge can of White-Out and correct all 74,000 papers?

There has been more than one instance when I wish I could do exactly that. I still remember the time we did a special section for the Long Beach Opera – a 10th anniversary or something, I don't recall – and misspelled the name of the featured opera on the front cover.

It didn't matter that the opera folks had signed off on that very cover, with. It was a mistake, and we ended up reprinting a bunch of the sections just so the opera could have some that were right. My stomach was upset for a week.

If anything, it is even more painful when you make a mistake when trying to do something good. I swear that last week I was trying to honor the folks who make it just a little easier on our students.

But a fair segment of those folks now will remember this as the time that Gazette guy gave someone else credit for their good work. And that is, indeed, painful.

I'm sorry, ladies. Truly I am.

EVERYONE LIKES A travel story, right? Well, at least it makes for a fairly entertaining column if there are enough disasters the readers can watch, but don't have to experience. This entire story is true, by the way.

Oct. 13, 2010

Somebody once said the excitement of a trip is not just the destination, but also the getting there.

Boy, howdy. Last week, personal business took me to Tulsa, Okla. I foolishly posted on Facebook that I was heading for the wild and wooly west, sealing my fate. The getting there was indeed an adventure.

I was driving a car back, so we (Maria came along) booked one-way flights to Tulsa. It comes as a surprise, I know, but there aren't too many options when you're trying to get to Oklahoma from Los Angeles. I didn't want to shell out for a charter flight, so I booked a late-night excursion on that airline that throws peanuts but doesn't charge for bags (we only had carry-on stuff, so lost that benefit).

The best I could do was a plane change in Denver. Ever notice how those Midwestern cities stick together? We had 45 minutes to make connections, so I was comfortable.

At least I was until the counter clerk announced the plane would be an hour late coming in to LAX. No explanation beyond a delay in getting out of Reno.

I rush up to the counter. "Oh, they'll hold your plane in Denver," the smiling attendant reassured me. "Connections to Tulsa and Oklahoma City will be waiting."

Sit back down. Then the plane was only half an hour late. Then it was back to an hour.

But it arrived, and we all rushed on. The pilot was backing away from the gate before the door closed, determined to make up time.

He did – we began our descent just more than 30 minutes past due. Only we stopped descending at around 5,000 feet.

The third time I saw the same set of lights out the window, I turned to Maria and said, "I think something's wrong."

Literally seconds later, the pilot got on the intercom.

"Sorry, folks, but we've been having a little problem with one of the flaps. We think everything's fine now, so we're going to land."

"We Think?"

But we made it. An hour after the flight to Tulsa was supposed to leave. We power walk down the concourse and march onto a plane full of people staring at us. They were not happy.

"Don't worry," I whispered to Maria. "There must be more people coming to make this connection."

Nope. A plane full of people had sat there for more than 30 minutes. For us. Not a good feeling.

Long story longer, we got into Tulsa at about 11:30 p.m. I call the motel, ask for the shuttle to pick us up.

"Okay," the desk clerk said. "But we just had a homicide here. I'm not sure how soon I can get the van out."

The room was already paid for, and I was not anxious to look for another motel in a strange city at midnight. I say we'll still come and check in.

Detectives were interviewing motel employees when we arrived, and the person helping us was distracted by the people in the back room watching and rewatcing the security video. But we got a room in a wing away from the crime scene, and collapsed in the bed.

Next morning, I turn on the faucet to take my daily ration of medication. No water comes out. Check the shower; nothing. The toilet tank is dry.

"Yeah, the pipes busted," the new desk clerk says when I call. "We're trying to get someone out to do somethin' about it."

We went next door to the Denny's for breakfast and a restroom visit. The waitress, Reba (I swear that was her name), knew all about the shooting.

"Two dead, a third in critical," she nodded sagely. "Pretty sure it was drugs."

An hour later, we were on about our business, which actually went pretty smoothly. The trip home was another story, but I won't bore you.

Suffice it to say, half the adventure is getting there.

ABOUT THE LIFE I LEAD

IDENTITY ISSUES ARE the bane of the 21st Century. Computers tell each other who we are, allowing everything from identity theft to mistaken identity, like this story. It took a good three months and at least one "do-over" to straighten it out.

Oct. 10, 2010

>The Car Odyssey, Part Two.
>I bet you thought I was going to write about the 1,500-mile drive from Tulsa, Okla., to Long Beach, Calif., didn't you?
>Well, there were a few interesting moments, like the Texas steak or talking my way out of a speeding ticket, but there really wasn't all that much to write about.
>Until I got home – and found out I was dead.
>Let me back up a bit. I've been relatively fortunate with my financial identity – no ID theft or lost cards, only one situation where someone made unauthorized charges. I do admit to stretching that credit at times, and my credit score doesn't compare with my SAT, but I don't have bill collectors calling or red stickers on my statements, either.
>That's just to establish my bonafides. Now on with the story.
>When I got home, I wanted to get the car in my name only to spare the relative I had cosigned from any further concern. That seemed like an easy request to me, but the credit union holding the loan felt otherwise. They couldn't just drop a name – the loan had to be refinanced.
>No problem, I thought. I was good enough to lend the money to two years ago, and there hadn't been any late payments.
>"Let me just put you on hold while I check your credit rating, okay?" the sweet young lady on the other end of the line said. "It won't take long at all."
>I went through 25 emails while I waited, so the time wasn't wasted. I was still feeling pretty good. Then she got back on the line.

"I'm sorry, sir (I hate it when I'm called sir), but we have a slight problem," she said.

"Problem?" I replied. "How's that?"

"Well, sir, it seems you are deceased," came the answer.

"You're talking to me, right?" I replied. "I sound at least sort of alive, don't I?"

"Of course, sir," she offered brightly. "It's just that the credit bureaus are listing you as deceased. They won't give us a credit rating."

And I immediately went from Tulsa, Hell, to Credit Bureau, Hell. It was a very quick trip.

Of course, the problem was obvious. My dad, who died about 18 months ago, and I have the same name. He was Harry Mack Saltzgaver III and in a fit of fiendish payback, made me a IV. A couple of credit card companies had given up on attempts to collect balances from his non-existent estate, and reported them closed due to his death.

Only those little notes went on my credit report.

Now the three credit bureaus all make a big deal about how willing they are to correct any errors, right? But the trick is, you've got to talk to someone. And that is virtually impossible.

I called the number for one of the bureaus and went directly to a phone advertisement for a credit repair company. I opted for the online option, filing a dispute on the website.

Tried a second bureau and, after furiously pounding on the zero on the phone for a good 30 seconds, actually got to speak to a person. He said his name was Jason. His Indian accent was so thick I could hardly understand him. After 10 minutes, I said I'd check their website.

The third bureau's representative actually found where it said I was deceased. "Okay, we'll file that dispute," she said. "You should hear from us in 30 or 45 days."

Then the credit union called.

"I'm sorry, but we can't extend you credit at this time," another sweet lady said.

"But I'm already paying on the loan," I replied. "I just want it in my own name. It makes no sense."

"I know, sir, but you're reported as deceased," she offered in an incredibly patient tone. "There's nothing I can do."

At last check, the credit bureaus still say I'm dead. How can I prove I'm alive?

Wait. If I'm dead, I don't have to pay those bills, right? Right, credit union lady?

There has been no reply.

CALL IT INTIMATIONS of mortality. Realizing that you are middle-aged – or past middle-aged – can come as a shock. But it can come as a joy, too.

Nov. 23, 1010

I guess it's a sign that I'm finally accepting my age.

You know how your self-image often is totally at odds with the reality that faces you in the mirror? I still consider myself a young buck. That's why I continue to take on things like splitting wood and climbing precarious ladders to hang Christmas lights.

In my heart of hearts, I refuse to believe that I'm old enough to carry an AARP card, or get a senior discount at the movies (she didn't even ask to see proof!). I try hard to keep up with the latest things so I can keep up with the newsroom conversation, where the average age is less than half my own.

But when son Alex uttered the latest indication of just how old I am during his visit last week, there wasn't an iota of denial. In fact, I was overjoyed.

All he said was, "You're going to be a grandpa."

Now I need to hasten to add here that I am, in most ways, already a grandpa. Maria's middle daughter, Charlotte, has blessed us with one granddaughter (Josephine, or Jo-Jo) and is carrying her second child as we speak. I walked Charlotte down the aisle, and certainly consider her a daughter.

Then there's Erik, our surrogate grandchild. The child of a friend of another daughter, we've been in his life since infancy. I've been Grandpa Harry to him for a decade now.

But at the risk of becoming the Juan Williams of the adoption society, there's just something about flesh and blood. Alex is my only son – my only child. When it comes to direct bloodlines, he is my only chance to carry on.

Alex and his wife, Lynn, have been trying to get pregnant for better than two years. I know, I know – that's what young couples do. But it got serious a couple of years ago, when doctors confirmed that the natural approach likely wouldn't result in a child.

Before you ask, yes, we did have the adoption conversation. They agreed that it was an alternative, but said they wanted to explore other avenues to have their own first.

Alex was honest about it. He said he knew it sounded selfish, but he wanted a child that was truly a part of them, physically as well as emotionally.

That meant expensive – and uncomfortable, at least for Lynn – procedures for them, and plenty of prayer for us. The pressure was intense. I personally think it was that pressure that caused the first effort to fail.

Worse, there's no money-back guarantee when it comes to in vitro fertilization procedures. The kids were out several thousand dollars with nothing to show for it.

It took six months for them to even begin talking about trying again. And this time around, beyond saying they were trying, they refused to provide further details. No procedure updates, no news at all.

Until last week. Lynn's seven weeks along, and Alex had a copy of the ultrasound on his iPhone. Not much to see, but hearing that heartbeat sent a tingle up my spine.

Clearly, I had absolutely nothing to do with the creation of this new life (unless you believe in the power of prayer). Yet I was proud. Very proud. Figure that one out.

We still have to go through the helpless feeling of waiting for a healthy baby to emerge, and if anything, those prayers are going to pick up the pace (for Charlotte too).

But I'm very comfortable now with the thought of grandpa-ism – something I was far too young for just a few days ago. In fact, I'm thankful. Very thankful.

It is a happy Thanksgiving for me. I hope it is for you, too.

THE RAPIDLY CHANGING world of technology is a given in our world today. Still, it is a good exercise to pause once in a while to notice just how rapid that change is happening.

Add the very special topic of a grandchild, and this turned into a very special column.

Feb. 17, 2011

"It's a girl! It's a healthy baby girl!"

That was son Alex on the phone on Monday. He was seriously excited, as any expectant father should be.

Expectant? That's right. Despite use of the phrase that usually accompanies a birth, young Alex still has to wait five months before he can hold his first child (my grandchild) in his hands.

His exclamations came, of course, from an ultrasound. It is just one of the many modern technologies that didn't exist just a generation ago.

Oh, there were ultrasounds when Alex was born. But they were pretty sketchy in terms of results, very expensive and seldom used. I don't recall if his mom had even one, although I do remember we knew he was a going to be a boy.

Lynn, the mom-to-be, already has had four ultrasounds. They've sent us pictures where we could see the fetus, and a video where we could hear the heartbeat. Wicked cool, as the saying goes.

Back in my day, when we used to walk four miles to and from school, in snow, and uphill both ways, this marvelous technology was nothing but a dream. The first thing you did when a baby was born was to count all the fingers and toes, just to make sure they all were there.

Seriously, the health of a newborn was always a concern, as little as three decades ago. Birth defects were called that specifically because they were detected at birth.

These days, technology allows a window into the womb, and much more. Just this week, a story hit the wires about a fetal surgery that successfully treated Spina Bifida, one of the more serious birth defects. We did a story just a couple of weeks ago about the successful treatment of fetuses in HIV-positive mothers to allow them to avoid infection with the disease.

Amazing.

In fact, if it weren't for modern technology, we wouldn't be talking today about a Saltzgaver grandchild. Due to medical circumstances, Alex and Lynn had to resort to artificial insemination in order to get pregnant.

That's not a source of shame, by the way. It is a source of pride and amazement, at least to me. Amazement that such a thing is possible, and pride that my son and his wife are so willing to become parents that they have put up with all the physical and financial sacrifices that it involved.

I'm proud that my boy was more concerned about the baby's health than its gender. And I'm amazed that doctors can say with confidence a full five months before birth that this child will be free of the challenges of mental or physical disability.

Some of my more fundamentalist friends might be squirming a bit about now, what with all of this human intervention into creation of life. But I have to say that I see this as yet another miracle.

As far as I'm concerned, it is divine intervention that has allowed this precious life to come into being. God has given us the gift of our intellect, and expects us to use it. That's exactly what these doctors, and those who discovered the technologies involved, are doing.

This child is a blessing.

That would make any God smile.

MORE OFTEN THAN not, when I try to save money it ends up costing me. Sometimes it cost money, but more often, it cost in pain. Readers seem to love it when it costs pain – this column got lots of comments.

March 17, 2011

>It hurts every time I move.
>That's the price I pay for being cheap. I'm paying double, because I'm both cheap and getting too old for this stuff.
>Let me tell you the exact source of this particular whine. It's a bit of a tale, so get comfortable.
>When I first moved into the 1940s house more than a decade ago, one of the biggest selling points was the existence of three large, mature trees. Trees and a big backyard sort of go with the territory when you buy a home in North Long Beach.
>I realized that trees grow, and that you sometimes need to trim them, so I rushed right out and bought a 16-foot industrial strength ladder. The first time I trimmed branches, it was not a big deal – I was in my 40s, in less than jock shape but not in the post-heart attack closing-in on 60 shape I'm in now.
>Even the pitched roof wasn't too big a problem. My balance was pretty good.
>But that 16-foot ladder didn't reach to the higher branches of any of my big trees, even back then. I was able to get by for a few years, but finally broke down four or five years ago and hired a real tree trimmer.
>His crew did a great job, finishing in one day and mulching up all the branches so they could take them away. It was like a really close tree haircut.
>That close haircut has lasted pretty well, but last summer was a good growing season for the trees. The sycamore is now tall enough that its growth really doesn't impact much on the ground – and it is smack in the middle of the front yard. But the other two

big boys are along the side of the house, and branches tend to hang over into the neighbor's yard and onto the roof.

So I decided to do something about it last weekend. I didn't have the extra $400 or so the tree trimmers wanted, so I had little choice but to do what I could on my own. At least that's what I convinced myself.

So the big ladder came off the garage wall for the first time in at least a half-dozen years. I started in the backyard so no one could see if (make that when) I made some awkward move.

At least I had enough sense not to tackle big limbs with a chainsaw – my lumberjack days might have been 30-some years ago, but I learned enough then to recognize danger when I saw it. I stuck with my big pruning branch cutters and left anything bigger than a couple of inches around alone.

Still, I had to get as much as I could, and that meant stretching precariously off the top of the ladder to get the blade around that 18-foot-high branch that trailed nearly to the ground. Remember that these days, simply holding my arms above my head for a minute is considered exercise.

What I want to know, though, is how my roof got steeper in the last 10 years. When I stepped onto the shingles, I started looking around for the pitons to climb to the top.

The limbs I had to cut there weren't that big. But I do think that the work was more muscle-straining than what I did on the ladder. It has something to do with the adrenaline generated by reaching over the edge of a 30-degree (felt like 60-degree) roof to cut a branch two feet away.

But I got it done, and without falling, no less. I only have one scratch on my face, and the branch that hit me on the head didn't even rip my hat.

I even thought I had survived without serious harm when I woke up Sunday with little soreness. Silly me. The nerve endings were just gathering strength. By the time I came to work Monday, even my fingers hurt.

The trees look okay, and my neighbor isn't giving me dirty looks any more. I still have a pile of limbs in the backyard, but I'll deal with them later – when I feel young again.

And I'll start saving up now for that close tree haircut next year. I'm getting too old for this stuff.

ABOUT THE LIFE I LEAD

BEING THE TOPIC of columns comes with the territory when you're a member of my family. But I've always been very careful not to make too much fun of relatives – particularly wives. It's not good for the homelife, if you know what I mean. This gentle ribbing is about as far as it usually went.

April 14, 2011

There's something about three generations.

I've said it before. Without a doubt, the best times I've ever had playing golf were when I managed to get my son and my father together on the same course at the same time.

Dad died two years ago, so that isn't going to happen anymore. But those memories will never die.

For the last week, I've been watching Maria experience the three-generation thing. Her middle daughter, Charlotte, came out for a surprise visit with her own daughter, 3-year-old Josephine.

Charlotte's expecting again, with a boy due in July. That will be plenty of fun, too, but this time with daughter and granddaughter is special.

Maria dotes on her granddaughter – always has. That's no surprise. She has a heart for small children and animals. If you look up caregiver in the dictionary, there she is, with a baby on one side and a dog on the other.

Truth be told, Charlotte's enjoying this, and taking full advantage. Grandma's cooking the meals, giving the baths, rocking Jo-Jo to sleep. Pregnant mom is pleased to take a load off, literally.

I already have a ton of pictures of the three of them together. The family resemblance is striking – pretty blondes, all.

The resemblance is more than physical. Don't tell her I said so, but Josephine shows every sign of being just as picky (that's polite for obsessive) about how things are placed and how the food is served as her mother and grandmother.

Case in point – we decided to brave a restaurant. Josephine

got mini-hot dogs.

First, the wieners had to come out of the little hot dog buns. During that process, one of the dogs accidentally touched the pool of catsup on the plate to accompany the French fries.

It took three napkins to clean the hotdog sufficiently before the first bite could be taken.

No big deal, I know. I'm just saying ...

You can obviously have three generations without being all male or all female, and my son and I will start down that road later this year (Alex and Lynn also are expecting in July, but it will be a little girl). I just think there is a special bond when it's all guys or all gals.

For example, all three of the girls can be in the same room together in various stages of undress, and there's nothing uncomfortable about it. Josephine is as innocent as they come, but she already knows to "cover up" when grandpa's around.

There are the common interests, too. The girls all pay attention to their hair. I can't participate in that conversation, even if I did have any – hair, that is. And we'll just ignore the fingernails, okay?

Maria has a long stretch of three-generation bonding ahead, and she's looking forward to it. I can tell. They are making memories, and there's nothing better than that.

I CAN SAY now that this particular adventure was one of the scariest I've experienced. I was certain I was going to fall off the roof and/or the ladder, and I was all alone. Somehow, I avoided the fall, and it ended up making a pretty decent story.

May 19, 2011

I headed to St. George, Utah, last weekend fully prepared to celebrate my father's memory in the third annual Harry Saltzgaver Memorial Golf Tournament.

After he died, his Elks Lodge began the tournament to raise money for its golf scholarships – a program Dad began. I've been a supporter since the beginning.

But shortly after I passed through Las Vegas, I received a call. Due to a series of unfortunate circumstances, the tournament was being postponed.

I soldiered on, and completed the journey to St. George. I had another way to honor my father's memory – a job I was planning in addition to the golf tournament anyway.

I became intimately involved with my father's ladder.

I know, I know. It sounds incestuous, doesn't it? But there's a good, if somewhat convoluted, explanation.

As the oldest son, I was the executor of my father's estate. That estate consisted primarily of credit card debts, some personal property (I got the recliner) and the mortgage on his home, a modular located in a 55 and older community.

Dad had the temerity to leave me with this responsibility right in the middle of the home mortgage crisis, so the mortgage was under water. I should have handled the house just like I handled the rest of his responsibilities – give it back to the bank. But one of his friends had a father who needed a place to live, so I kept the place and rented it to him.

Of course, the bank wouldn't let me take the mortgage over – I wasn't going to live there, and my credit rating is far south of the perfection now required to get a new loan. So the estate remains open, and the executor (me) remains responsible for the asset.

Which brings us to last weekend. I had received a cryptic call from the Homeowners Association saying that the house "needed paint and had some rotting wood." I had plans of doing a reconnaissance on Saturday, then playing in the tournament on Sunday.

When I got to the house, though, it was clear the message was in regards to some flaking paint on the trim and five or six pieces of sprinkler-damaged wood. Clearly it was something within my limited home repair capabilities, and I could save maybe a grand by doing it myself.

Is this starting to sound familiar? Yes, yet another Saltzgaver home repair adventure.

I'll have you know I am getting better. It only took two trips to Home Depot to complete the job (okay, I did have to improvise for the paint rags, but hey).

I had left some of Dad's tools in the garage, including an extension ladder he had clearly used for previous paint jobs. It was vital, since the majority of the trim was 10 to 15 feet above the ground.

Long story short, I spent the next two days going up and down that ladder, one paint roller full at a time. I did figure out by the second day how to bring a cup of paint along with the brush for the touchup work, but the paint pan and the ladder weren't compatible (besides, I had to move the ladder every roller full or two anyway).

I quickly employed all of my stretching techniques to limit the number of ladder moves. No one was watching, so I broke all the safety rules, hanging on with one hand and one foot 10 rungs off the ground while I stretched to reach the farthest corner. God truly does protect fools.

The wind was picking up as I extended the ladder to its full height Sunday afternoon to get to the stupid peak the stupid home manufacturers put on the stupid house. I had this nasty Charlie

Brown kite feeling as I crawled onto the roof, away from my dearly beloved ladder. Have you ever tried to paint while lying on your stomach? Turns out I have that skill.

I spent an extra 10 minutes on that roof, just trying to summon the courage to remount my trusty ladder in the 30 mph breeze. But she proved true and steady, and I made it back to the ground.

I now have bruises in places where I didn't know you could bruise, as a direct result of my relationship with that ladder. Still, a job is done. It undoubtedly is much messier than what Dad would have done, but I did it all by myself – just like he did.

That's honoring his memory, at least in the Saltzgaver tradition. Love you, Dad.

Next time, though, let's play golf.

20 YEARS OF SALT

THERE ARE TWO things you can write about and virtually guarantee a positive response – kids and pets (that's true of front page pictures, too). It gets even better when the kids are grandkids. See if you agree.

July 13, 2011

Nine pounds even. Twenty-one inches long. Stout, with strong lungs.

Mekhi (German for Mike) Busch entered the world of air-breathing humans just after 2 a.m. Monday, July 11. He was a week overdue – guess he must have heard about the debt ceiling debacle or something.

Mekhi's mom, Charlotte, is my wife Maria's middle daughter. This is her second child – Josephine is 3 years old and will undoubtedly terrorize her little brother for at least the first decade of his life.

While Mekhi carries none of my DNA, there's little doubt that he is my grandchild. The proof is I was showing off a dark, sort-of blurry picture of him on my phone in between shots at Monday's Mayor's Trophy golf tournament. I'm resisting posting it on my Facebook page, but it's undoubtedly better than the portrait that's up there now – I'm the subject of that one.

If this keeps up, I'm going to have to admit I'm not a kid any more.

And it is going to keep up. My son Alex's wife, Lynn, already is four days overdue as I write this. Her doctor has promised that the baby girl will be born by Friday even if the labor has to be induced. We'll see – these kids clearly have reluctance to join us, and probably for good cause.

If you didn't notice, I have not called Baby Girl Saltzgaver by name. It's because I can't – Alex and Lynn have refused to tell anyone what they plan to name the child. They'll let the decision be known after the ink is dry on the birth certificate and no one can try to talk them into changing the name.

That's probably not a bad idea. I'm not one to hassle young parents about their naming decisions, but I'm undoubtedly in the minority. I know I've already been threatened with bodily harm if I slip and call Mekhi Mikey, or some other derivative (there's little doubt I'll mess it up). I'm betting Charlotte and Mike have taken some guff.

I've been told that my parents had been pretty much ordered to call me Harriet if I turned out to be a girl – I was born long before doctors could tell what gender a fetus was going to be – because my dad, his dad and his granddad were all named Harry. My mother, who was the first-borne in her family, was named Claudia because her dad was named Claude. There's one of those for most names.

That stuff comes directly from family pressure, and it's worse these days. Not because kids these days pay so much attention to their parents' wishes (far from it), but because there are more of us. For good or ill, people are more likely to be divorced today. Mekhi has three sets of grandparents – two full sets and an extra grandpa.

Baby Girl Saltzgaver will have four full sets of grandparents. That no doubt will make for some great hauls for her come Christmas and her birthday, but it will put plenty of pressure and her mom and dad. I'm a little surprised Alex and Lynn haven't imposed a visitor time limit, or maybe a perimeter fence.

I'm of the mind that a kid can't have too many grandparents, too many people to love them. I've written before about our "fake" grandson, Erik, who is grandson by all but blood, so I think I live out that belief.

But I draw the line at telling the parents, my kids, how to raise their kids, or even what to name them, for that matter. So Alex and Lynn could have told me what the name is going to be. Honest, I wouldn't have said a word.

But son, do you really think it's a good idea to paint the nursery that color? And I'm telling you that idea of having a bassinet in your bedroom is going to cause you grief. But I like the idea of letting her hair grow for at least the first five years or so.

What do you mean you have another call? Grandpa Who? I'm Grandpa.

Want to see some pictures?

ABOUT THE LIFE I LEAD

WRITING ABOUT YOUR mistakes is a time-honored way to humanize yourself to your readers. I kept this particular "mistake" at least semi-private for 10 years. That was at least partially due to the proximity of the 9/11 terrorist attacks. My little issue certainly paled by comparison.

Then there was the fact that I wanted to make sure my sobriety took. I figured 10 years was about right.

Sept. 7, 2011

I am well aware that 9/11 means many things to many people, and that you undoubtedly will read many memories of that day before the coming weekend is over.

But I'm going to ask you to read a memory of Sept. 13, 2011. I hope you don't mind.

This story starts on Sept. 11, 2001, as so many things did. If you recall, that was a Tuesday – deadline day for the Grunion Gazette.

Then-publisher and owner John Blowitz woke me shortly before 6 a.m. with that now-dreaded phrase, "Turn your TV on."

That started a very long day. We are a community weekly, and frankly, we're not geared up for coverage of national or international tragedy.

But it was clear from the start that we couldn't ignore the terrorist attacks. So we went to work, and tried to cover the biggest news of the decade our way – locally.

With stellar efforts from Kurt Helin and Amy Bentley-Smith (both have since moved on to other endeavors), we put together what I still consider to be one of the finest Grunions ever. It had news and approaches that no one else had, and that were important to our readers.

As I said, though, this story isn't about that day – it's about the Thursday that followed.

The paper made it out on the street in good shape. We were

all still reeling from events, but we were moving on.

My good friend Randy Gordon, president and CEO of the Long Beach Chamber of Commerce, had made a tough call, and decided that the Chamber's annual golf tournament would go on as scheduled. I think he made the right call – it was the first instance of not letting the terrorists win by altering our lives.

Only about two-thirds of the scheduled players showed up, but I was one of them. I deserved a little relaxation, even a little escape.

So when the guys I had been paired with (I was a guest, and didn't know them), stocked their cart with a couple of six packs and offered me a beer, I said sure. I grabbed another one from the tub on the tee box at the second hole we played, and when the tequila shot hole came around, I wasn't shy.

You can probably see where this is going. I didn't keep count, but I can pretty much guarantee that I had more beers than I had good shots – golf shots, I mean.

I wasn't hurting anyone, and I wasn't sloppy or anything. I was maintaining pretty well, and there was enough food on the course to absorb at least some of the alcohol.

When I made it back to the clubhouse, I was feeling no pain. But it wouldn't have been courteous of me to turn down the drink a friend offered, now would it? He doesn't know it to this day, but that drink with Phil was a momentous one.

I didn't stay for dinner – I was supposed to pick someone up. So I threw my clubs in the trunk and took off, not even stopping to take off my golf shoes.

They pulled me over just two intersections from the golf course. Actually, I had already pulled over, due to a little fender bender. I didn't even attempt to argue when they told me to put my hands behind my back.

I'm not going to talk about what police were doing worrying about drunk drivers two days after a terrorist attack. I'm certainly not going to argue that I deserved a break.

ABOUT THE LIFE I LEAD

But I got a break. Oh, I didn't get out of the DUI, or the consequences. But that arrest was the 2x4 to the head that I needed from God to get my act together, pray and seek help.

Between God and an outfit called AA, that craving for alcohol has disappeared. That drink with Phil was my last – at least my last for the last 10 years. That's almost as important as the fact that I've stayed sober today.

This memory isn't meant to celebrate what a great guy I am, what a great program AA is or how important God is in my life (although two of the three are definitely true). Like so many memories of that week 10 years ago, it's meant to provide a lesson for living today.

Don't wait for the 2x4. If you have trouble, seek help before it is forced on you, or you hurt someone.

Make a memory. A good one.

Part FOUR
All About Long Beach

ALL ABOUT LONG BEACH

EARLY IN MY time in Long Beach, I still felt compelled to explain the importance of community newspapers. It may have been an ego thing — trying to justify going back to the weekly after a decade in dailies. But the fact remained, then and now, that the community paper fills an important role.

I used a panel in front of the city's arts community to make the point just seven months after arriving in town.

Oct. 22, 1992

I had the honor to sit on a panel last week with several high-powered art types.

The occasion was a Public Corporation for the Arts workshop for artists. The idea was to explain how newspapers and critics worked, and to give the artists some idea of how they could publicize their work.

High-powered doesn't really do justice to the other panelists. As I sat down, Peter Plagens, the art critic for Newsweek, took the chair on the other end of the table. Christopher Knight, the L.A. times' art critic, sat down next to me, resplendent in a red jacket. The Press-Telegram sent managing editor Rich Archbold just to compete.

As I said, I was honored to appear with these heavy hitters. I also discovered again why I decided to return to community newspapers after nearly a decade trying to climb the corporate ladder of journalism.

But the fact is, one of the main things that came out of the workshop, is that our newspapers serve a purpose the big boys can't touch. It's sad reality that 95% of those artists will never receive a notice in Newsweek, and the figure isn't much lower for the L.A. Times.

On the other hand, up to 95% of those attending last week probably will appear in the Grunion or Downtown Gazette. It could be a subject of a feature story. It more likely will be as a notice of a show. But one way or another, we will let the community know what those folks are doing.

That's what I see as a primary function of community newspapers. No, not to provide publicity for artists; but to let the readers know what is available for them.

That goal extends to every other community group in the city. That's why we run a weekly calendar, and why most of our stories talk about what is going to happen, not what has happened.

And there is always more than enough going on in Long Beach to fill the newspaper with events. It's one of the reasons I enjoy living here.

It's also one of the reasons my co-workers think I'm an ogre when it's time to decide what goes in the paper and what doesn't make it. Because we only have so much space, and every week, someone's event has to be left out.

Those decisions aren't made arbitrarily or spitefully. I try my best to get the news in that the most people will be interested in.

I know it is frustrating to not get notice for an event or a cause you have worked hard on. I'd like to think that seldom happens to people involved in local (as in Belmont Shore, downtown, east Long Beach) events.

It makes me feel good to know we accomplish the goal of letting our readers know what's available out there more often than not. And it gives me pain when I'm unable to give a deserving group or individual the coverage they deserve.

In the end, all I can say is what I said to the artists – don't give up, and don't take it personally if your item didn't make it this week.

There's another edition next week.

ALL ABOUT LONG BEACH

I GREW UP playing baseball. It was my salvation from being a brainy geek. I started playing when I was 7, and had many great moments; even played a couple of years in college.

But I never went to the Little League World Series. It was, to say the least, a huge story when Long Beach won two titles in a row.

Sept. 2, 1993

World champions. National television exposure. Front-page treatment. Ticker tape parades.

And, in a couple of weeks, the sixth grade.

Hurrah for the Long Beach Little League All-stars.

Unless you've been on a trip to Zimbabwe for the last week, you know the story by now. Long Beach's young baseball players have conquered the world on their own field of dreams.

The team won the world title for the second year in a row – a feat unequalled by any other U.S. team. And this year, they won it on the field, rather than having it turned over to them after a cheating scandal was uncovered in the Philippines.

I wondered last year how anyone could turn a game into something worth an international scandal. And I'm still ambivalent about the attention – and pressure – showered on these children.

And they are children, after all. They're 11 and 12 years old. Aside from the admittedly unique specimen of Sean Burroughs, most weigh less than 100 pounds soaking wet.

Yet to hear the politicians – and, it's true, a fair share of the media – these youngsters are the salvation of the city. They are seen as a bright, shining light in a time dominated by stories of crime, recession and worry about the direction of youth.

Mixed in the millions of words written about the Beach Boys in the last week was an allegory comparing them to what should be a goal for youth today – a group striving together with teamwork, following the rules, counting on hard work and skill to carry the day. They did just that, and should be applauded for it.

I applauded along with the rest of the city when Jeremy Hess got the winning hit. My heart was in my throat, along with the rest of the city, Tuesday when the team received a hero's welcome.

But a small voice in the back of my head keeps whispering. It asks, "How much pressure can 12-year-old shoulders bear?"

I've been involved with Little League baseball ever since I can remember. I started playing when I was 7, and my glove and bat helped pay my way through college. I coached teams, I umpired for years and I helped administer one of the premier programs in Colorado.

I remember screaming myself hoarse as my son Alex struck out the side to win a league championship game. I've spent hours extolling the virtues of sports as builders of character for winners and losers alike.

So why was it I was at a loss for an explanation when Reetz asked, "How can they do that to little boys?" as we watched tears roll down the cheeks of a strike-out victim last Saturday? Why could I only agree with her about how painful it must be for the Panamanian pitcher being pulled instead of explaining to her the baseball strategy behind the move?

Because they're just kids.

The Beach Boys are experiencing an extended 15 minutes of fame more intense than what most people experience in their entire lives. I don't want to take anything away from that. I hope they all savor every moment in the limelight. They deserve to celebrate success, and we need to celebrate our youngsters accomplishing something positive.

But I hope their parents and teachers are strong enough to provide some balance – to be able to say this victory is a beginning, not an end. To be able to take this amazing success and make it the start of 14 successful lives.

Baseball, and competitive sport, is often an allegory for life –

there are winners and there are losers. I suspect the Beach Boys will do just fine in the bigger game – they're winners.

But as we celebrate, let's try to remember. They really are just kids.

I AM WELL aware that term limits remain popular with voters, and even some political types. I'd contend that the current mess the state is in is due, in large part, to those same term limits. On a local level, the ultra-partisan, always looking for the next office approach seen from many elected leaders has made city business – and a citywide perspective – a distant second in priorities.

At least that's how I see the ramifications of term limits. This is the take I had after Long Beach voters first passed term limits for the City Council.

June 23, 1994

Long Beach residents are about to discover what they have wrought, at least in the political arena.

I'm not talking about the new council, with its three new members and a new mayor – although that's going to be mighty interesting to watch. I'm speaking about the political "reforms" the electorate has put in place.

More specifically, I'm talking about the two-term limit imposed on council members two years ago. The way the change to the city charter was worded, the city now has two lame-duck council members – even though they still have four years to serve. Both Third District Councilman Doug Drummond and the Fifth District's Les Robbins are precluded from running for another term in 1998.

Which means, in the world of politics, that they no longer have to base their actions on whether or not it will upset the voters enough to oust them. Or at least they no longer have to tailor their decisions to please just the folks in their own district.

I'm not suggesting either Drummond or Robbins are going to become loose cannons, or that they aren't going to represent their districts to the best of their ability. On the contrary. Knowing both men, they will make it a point of honor.

But the fact remains, when 1998 rolls around, their futures

won't be in the hands of the constituents they're now sworn to represent.

That situation offers some pluses. They can take unpopular stands without fear of voter retaliation (at least if a try for higher office is not a factor), and these are times when some unpopular decisions are going to have to be made. Look for Drummond and Robbins to take the heat for necessary cuts in the tough budgets of this and next year.

They also can offer straightforward analysis of situations without worrying about backlash (at least if they don't mind the phone calls and letters). A politician telling it like it is, rather than telling it like what the voters want to hear, could be refreshing, and enlightening.

But they also run the risk of becoming long-term lame ducks, more concerned with other things than council business. And if you don't think that has an impact on your future, tune in to the current budget deliberations.

Mayor Ernie Kell isn't even attending the budget sessions. He has turned the gavel over to Vice Mayor Jeff Kellogg and gone on to other things (including a second "Goods for Guns" attempt to get weapons off the street, to his credit).

Evan Braude, who will give up his First District seat, has attended some of the sessions, but has been awfully quiet. Warren Harwood, the defeated Ninth District councilman, and Ray Grabinski, who gave up his Seventh District seat to try for mayor, remain involved in the discussion. But Harwood is focusing on his own pet projects and vendettas. Give Grabinski credit – he continues to view the big picture, even if it is from his own perspective.

So five of the nine people (six of 10, if you count the mayor) responsible for approving the city's budget will not face the same voters for the same office again. As noted, that can be both good and bad. It's guaranteed it will have an impact on the city's path to the future, though.

One final note on term limits. Supporters said it was necessary to get new blood into city government. Come July 19, the new blood is there, with three new council members and a new mayor.

And not one of those changes was because of term limits. Makes you wonder, doesn't it?

A MURDER IN Belmont Shore is an almost never occurrence. The William Shadden murder had the added component of involving a prominent family. I wrote several stories and columns about it over more than two years. This was, I think, the best of the bunch.

Feb. 2, 1995

It has taken nearly two years.
One young life has been snuffed out. Two others are ruined. Three sets of families have been left with permanent scars in their hearts.
All for a bicycle.
To say it doesn't make much sense is the ultimate in understatement. But then, there is a lot in this violent world of today that doesn't make much sense.
I've followed the William Shadden case since the morning after Memorial Day 1993. That night, Shadden was gunned down by a couple of gang wannabes, allegedly trying to steal his bicycle as he rode home from work. I suspect the murder had as much to do with a couple of punks trying to prove their macho to the "real" gang members as anything else.
In the last two years, I've gotten to know William's parents, Tom and Sandi. They're a great couple. Before Memorial Day 1993, they could easily have been a poster family for the Great American Dream. Tom is a high-powered businessman; the family has a super Naples home; they were involved in yachting to the extent that Tom was a primary motivating force behind the creation of the U.S. Sailing Center.
We crossed paths at charity events. They are big boosters of the Long Beach Symphony Orchestra. They epitomized the type of resident that makes Long Beach work.
These days, it is Sandi who is best known to the public. She has taken the tragedy of her son's death and turned it into something positive – Citizens and Businesses Against Crime. To her

credit, this is no vigilante group demanding mindless punishment. It has worked to create drug-free zones around schools, helped purchase a law-enforcing dog for the police department and in general taken a proactive approach to trying to stop crime.

But the pain of the mother was apparent last week, when a teenager named Leif Taylor finally faced a judge for sentencing. Taylor was convicted of pulling the trigger that ended William Shadden's life. Taylor's family members, rather naturally, contend that he didn't do it. The jury decided otherwise.

And Sandi Shadden said Taylor deserved to die. An eye for an eye.

Judge Charles Sheldon didn't have that option. Taylor was a juvenile when the crime was committed, and it was a semi-stretch for the judicial system to even try him as an adult for the murder. His accomplice, Victor Rodriguez, languishes in a youth facility now and will be released when he turns 25 – because he was only 14 on Memorial Day 1993.

Sandi Shadden's plea did sway the judge, though. Despite favorable reports about Taylor from everyone beginning with friends and ending with the jailers who have come to know him over the last year, Sheldon said Taylor would spend the rest of his life behind bars with no possibility of parole.

It's a sure bet the sentence will be appealed – that's the way our justice system works these days. And Sandi and Tom will have to keep reliving the pain, going back to court again and again to either keep one perpetrator from being released on parole or to maintain the sentence of the other.

I can only hope that Sandi can continue to turn her pain into a positive force to help stop crime. I have boundless admiration for her strength in doing that – I fear I would become vengeful and destructive in the same position.

So I'll leave the work to her. And if there is anything I can do to help her, I will.

THE AQUARIUM OF the Pacific has become a Long Beach icon rivaling the Queen Mary in recognition. But, like any major endeavor, there were plenty of detractors. I wasn't one of them. When the aquarium opened in 1998, I tried to show why it was going to be popular, and important.

June 11, 2012

"Wow, fishes!"

That exclamation from a kindergartner rushing toward the Tropical Reef preview tank Sunday pretty much summed up the experience. After nearly two years of dust, toil and $117 million, the Long Beach Aquarium of the Pacific is ready to show off.

"Wow, fishes!"

It seemed fitting that a jackhammer punded away down by the new harbor as I joined the stream of charter members eager to get a sneak peek at our new jewel. This is, and will continue to be for some time, a work in progress.

But once I stepped past the ship's bow that graces the entrance (a not-so-subtle indicator I was going on a cruise through the Pacific), the construction zone feel faded away.

"Wow, fishes!"

By now, you've surely heard all the statistics — more than 10,000 animals (fish, birds and mammals combined), more than a million gallons of water, etc. It truly is an edifice of grand scale.

It you want to wax symbolic, the humungous blue whale sculpture in the lobby, combined with the three-story tall tank at the far end of the football field-sized Great Hall, serves as an apt metaphor for the vastness of the Pacific Ocean. The spacious room and its soft curves of staircases to the second floor evoke the feeling of floating without a speck of land on the horizon.

But let's get back to what is going to make the Aquarium of the Pacific a resounding success.

One small child saying, "Wow, fishes!"

While the grandeur of the aquarium, the surrounding Rainbow Harbor and, in the next couple of years, the Queensway Bay development will swell Long Beach with pride – and hopefully the city coffers with money – it's that child who will define the aquarium's true success.

It's all about providing that child with a chance to personally interact with the ocean environment. Stretch the child's age to between 3 and 100, then multiply him or her by about two million, and you've defined a successful first year at the Aquarium of the Pacific.

Warren Iliff and his staff have managed to keep those one-on-one encounters in the forefront as they have created this imposing edifice. Little touches like live labs and touch tanks at toddler level exist solely to serve the individual. Major architectural features such as curved glass and walk-in alcoves aim to let people have a true communion with the ocean around them.

I could go on for hours. Attention to detail – down to the mists of the Bering Sea and the lighting in the moon jelly exhibit – is exquisite. Fanciful touches – the fish imprints on the floor (and in the parking garage), the memorial bricks prominently displayed – all are designed to engage the individual, not herd the masses through.

When I walk through the aquarium doors, and I've done so several times already, I am that kindergartener. The thoughts can be complex, the feelings deep. But it still comes down to this:

"Wow, fishes!"

ALL ABOUT LONG BEACH

I'VE HAD MORE than my share of run-ins with Long Beach's own brand of self-proclaimed environmentalists over the years. I've outlasted most of them – they have had a tendency to move away after a few years of rabble-rousing.

I didn't necessarily oppose their environmental stances – it was their stubborn and never-ending delaying tactics that really got to me. There were many other instances of that approach, but the reuse of the Long Beach Naval Station was a prime example.

Dec. 3, 1998

When is enough enough? When does fighting the good fight become fighting the ridiculous fight?

I would submit that the folks railing against the demise of the Naval Station have long passed both boundaries. Come on, people. The game's over. Move on.

I guess it's my sports background, but I've always believed in doing your best during the game, then accepting the results, win or lose. Let me carry the analogy a little further.

When Pittsburgh lost the coin toss to Detroit on Thanksgiving Day (this is football, for you of the non-sporting ilk) on what was a blatant error by an official, the game went on. When Pittsburgh lost, there was lots of complaining, but no one suggested replaying the game.

When Naval Station opponents won in court and forced a second re-use study, they praised the judicial system to the skies. When the second study came back with essentially the same results – a port use for land in, of all places, the middle of a port – those same folks went back to court again. And again. And again.

Finally, the latest judge got tired of saying no and just waited them out. Lawsuits seeking to stop destruction of something that is already gone don't hold much water, even in this litigious society of ours.

Would they quit? Of course not. They hadn't got the answer they wanted — they were on the short end of the score.

But now they've managed to look absurd.

Okay, the Don Quixote thingh as a long and honored position in history. But the idea of asking the people of Long Beach to vote to rebuild historic buildings (yes, that is an oxymoron) has got to go down as one of the most fanciful windmills of all time. If Ken Larkey, the man who started the election push, has some magic key to pull this off, I assume a vote to restore the Pike's tattoo parlors is just around the corner.

Is it asking too much for a little perspective here?

There's no reason to suppose that Ann Cantrell and Colette Marie McLaughlin are seeking my advice, or will listen to what I have to suggest (although it is a virtual guarantee the letters will be in the mail the day this appears), but I've got to say this anyway. If you want people to give credence to what you have to say, don't smother it in offensive hyperbole.

I'm talking about McLaughlin's comparison of knocking down some buildings to the Tiananmen Square massacre — she did that in front of the City Council. I'm talking about Cantrell comparing her feelings after the demolition to her feelings when family members (mother and grandmother) died.

I don't pretend to know how these women feel. I do take offense to those types of comparisons, though, and suspect many others do, as well.

These women and others who have fought the good fight have incredible energy and an almost psychopathic dedication. It's a shame to see it wasted.

It's also a shame to see the amount of time, energy and resources they've forced so many others — from the city to the Navy to the courts — to waste. Constructive things went waiting while the windmill tilting went on.

There will be more games, folks. Promise. But this one's over.

Move on.

ALL ABOUT LONG BEACH

TRYING TO EXPLAIN why I decided early on to spend serious time on community efforts seemed at times easy – the paper was a community paper and I was a community guy – and at other times almost impossible. I have often been accused of taking the city's side in issues – I argue that I take the community's side.

In this case, I tried to co-op the reader into understanding that point of view.

June 3, 1999

I'm facing a bit of a dilemma, and I'm asking you, faithful reader, to help me out.

You see, next week I'm going to become the president of the board at the PCA – the Public Corporation for the Arts, for the acronym-challenged. The dilemma part comes at our annual meeting, where I'm expected to say a few words.

The operative word here is "few." I tried to write those "few" words the other day, and covered several pages with notes.

Now, I don't want to put the folks at the meeting to sleep with a 30-minute speech, but there's a whole bunch of things I want to say about the arts in Long Beach. So I came up with this solution. I'm going to ask you to read a chunk of it. Feel free to offer portions to cut. Here goes.

I feel extremely privileged to have the opportunity to help take the PCA and the arts community of Long Beach into the 21st Century.

My dream – I believe the dream of all of us here – is to reaffirm Long Beach as a place where the better half of the human soul shines brightly – a place where our artistic, our humanistic, nature overwhelms the negative and violent sliver of our community. I see a place where diverse cultures are celebrated, instead of set at odds. I see a city where youngsters learn the joy of creating art instead of the despair of gangs, drugs and ignorance.

The foundation for that dream has been laid both by the incredible talent with which this city has been blessed and by the great supporters we have behind the scenes. We've applauded as JoAnn Falletta led the Long Beach Symphony to new heights. We've cheered as Hal Nelson turned the dream of an expanded Museum of Art into a reality, as we have stood in awe of Robert Gumbiner's single-minded realization of his vision at the Museum of Latin American Art.

We've witnessed the resurgence of theater in Long Beach as the Edison Theatre opened as the new home for Howard Berman's incredible Cal Rep company, the venerable Long Beach Playhouse gave itself a spectacular makeover and now Shashin Desai and the International City Theatre's step into the spotlight as the resident theater company at the Performing Arts Center. The College of the Arts at Cal State Long Beach finally is beginning to get the recognition it deserves, and the seats are filling at the Carpenter Center, the Terrace Theater and our many other great venues.

I'm extremely fortunate in following two incredibly hard-working men as president of the PCA. Gordon Lentzner and Steve Horn, Jr. have prepared the foundation from which we can build. They continue a 22-year tradition of strong leadership at the PCA that I feel humbled in attempting to try to maintain.

In particular, Steve has paved the way for the city to consider increasing its support of the arts to $2 a person. Long Beach residents long have supported the arts, and we've been fortunate to maintain government support at a steady level during tough economic times, thanks largely to the help of City Managers James Hankla and Henry Toboada and Mayor Beverly O'Neill.

But now, as we enter the 21st Century, it is time to renew our commitment to that good side of human nature we call the arts with this modest increase in public support. I say modest because many of our country's cities spend much more than $2 a person per year on the arts, and without the talent that Long Beach boasts.

We're talking less money per person in a year than it costs to rent "Animal House" for a night, folks. Doesn't Long Beach, and Long Beach's soul, deserve at least that much?

I congratulate and thank you all for your individual support for the arts in Long Beach, and hope that you will continue to be supporters. I ask just one thing more – help convince our city leaders that we must be committed and supportive as a community, as well.

So, that's my speech. What do you think? Can you help?

HEALTH CARE CONSOLIDATION, like business consolidation in general, picked up speed at the turn of the century. It came to Long Beach in the form of closure of one of the city's three major hospitals. The way it was done, not necessarily the fact it was done, was a big bone of contention.

June 29, 2000

> The writing was on the wall.
> Too bad it wasn't in the mail, or over the phone.
> When Catholic Healthcare West announced last week that they were going to close Community Medical Center, "I told you so's," could be heard throughout the city. The rapidly changing and ever-less-profitable world of providing hospital health care had pointed in the direction of a closure from the day the religious/medical conglomerate purchased Community.
> Like it or not, closing Community is the fiscally responsible thing to do. Whether it is the socially responsible thing to do is entirely another question.
> But then, CHW has shown remarkably little social conscience, or even simple courtesy, in this fiasco. That's extremely upsetting, particularly coming from a religious-based organization supposedly dedicated to serving its fellow man and woman. But more about that later.
> As noted before, Community's closing came as no real surprise, at least to the people at all aware of the financial situation of Long Beach's hospitals. But the ham-handed way in which the closure announcement was handled gave it the feeling of a "midnight run" closing by a slightly sleazy business owner, leaving customers and creditors in the lurch.
> Last Thursday, a press release was being circulated before the mayor, the city manager or anyone else with authority in the city was contacted by CHW. Even the president of the board of trustees at St. Mary Medical Center – a CHW hospital opened

nearly a century ago by Catholic nuns – found out about it from the media.

The decision to close Community came from on high. No, not that high. A board of directors for the corporation made the call.

Who knows who made the decision not to seek help from the city, or even inform them of what was going on? Who decided to ignore the political and very real geographic concerns of closing the only major hospital and emergency room east of Atlantic Avenue?

What it comes down to is a group that had made its reputation as a compassionate, caring health care provider showed that it has become yet another of those mega-conglomerates that act as if they are omnipotent, acting in their own little world with no regard for the impact to those around them.

City officials now are scrambling to try to save at least a portion of Community. CHW will resist selling the hospital to someone else to operate – a prime motivation for the closure was cutting down the competition for patients. A restraining order likely will have little effect, because CHW already must go through a series of hearings and permits to close the hospital.

What might, and should, happen is a new use for the hospital campus. If a full-service emergency room is part of that plan, it would significantly ease the impact on east Long Beach residents. My personal preference would be to see some of that unused bed space turned into a gerontology center, serving the ever-increasing needs of our senior citizen population.

But whatever happens, CHW is going to have a devil of a time erasing the smirch on its religious-compassionate image. Perhaps the ones who will be hurt the most are those at St. Mary. The people there, from the saintly sisters to the janitors, continue to provide what they hope is compassionate health care.

But it is going to take a lot to convince Long Beach there is much God in a conglomerate that takes unilateral decisions based on the bottom line. I can't argue with the financial reasons for closing Community – I've seen the numbers and that writing was indeed on the wall. But I can argue with the way it was, and is, being handled.

That's just plain heartless.

AH, THE GOOD old days – back when a budget debate meant how much to spend on quality of life issues such as art support, not basic necessities like cops and parks. More ironic is the fact that this column was written a bare week before the 9-11 terrorist attacks.

To the city leadership's credit, they made good on their promise to the arts community. But the climax turned out to be a last hurrah. Here is how is sounded before the world changed.

September 6, 2001

About 27 months ago, I used this column to write a little speech. I was about to become chair of the board for the Public Corporation for the Arts. Well, I'm stepping down from that position next week, and I've got to give another speech. I'd like to try it out on you.

It's a wonderful time for arts and culture in Long Beach. In fact, it's a historic time.

The City Council has more than doubled its general support for the arts to $1.75 million. Led by Third District Councilman Frank Colonna (our hero!), the city will provide enough money to allow a plethora of artists and arts organizations to further improve the quality of life in Long Beach through art and culture.

Never before has this city made such a significant commitment to the arts. But, and this is a fair question, what does it mean to you, the resident?

To start, it will mean higher quality, and more stability, for the city's major arts organizations. Performances at the Long Beach Symphony, International City Theatre and Musical Theatre West will be further augmented by more community outreach. Exhibitions at the Long Beach Museum of Art and the Museum of Latin American Art will have the little something extra special a decent budget can provide, and more children and neighborhoods will experience art as programs grow.

On the other end of the scale, more individual artists in the growing Long Beach art community will find work through contracts with the PCA. That work will reach out into your neighborhood. It will touch your children.

Much the same can be said for those arts groups in the middle – the "mom and pop" organizations that are the backbone of the effort to bring art to Long Beach. Whether it's classical (such as the Long Beach Opera), experimental (my friends at the Found Theater), ethnic (such as the African-American Cultural Center) or community-based (think East Village Arts District and the fledging Long Beach Center for the Arts in Bixby Knolls), these are the folks that are in the art trenches. They touch you even when you're not looking.

Thanks to the City Council, our city's artists – performing, visual and everything in between – will have a chance to make Long Beach a better place. That's a definite win for each and every one of us who live here.

None of this would have happened without the artists and art supporters. In the past two years, I have watched the art community coalesce into a unified, significant force with a single mission. Even when things seemed bleak, they maintained their vision of improving our city through art.

Consider just a few of the major accomplishments in the past few years. Music & Art for the Millennium, a collaboration between the symphony and the Museum of Art, touched more than 100,000 youngsters. Smithsonian Week in Long Beach has become a national model for mixing art, culture and the nation's museum. Passport to Art in the Schools has jump-started a resurgence in art education.

The Museum of Art more than doubled its space with a stunning new gallery building. The East Village's dream of an art district is fast becoming reality. The symphony attracted an international star to replace the beloved JoAnn Falletta. Not one, but two top-notch theater companies have established themselves as regional draws, with ICT bringing theater lovers downtown and

MTW attracting musical theater fans to the Carpenter Center. The one-of-a-kind MoLAA has established an international reputation.

I could go on and on – and probably will when I actually give the speech. But you get the point.

We've made Long Beach a better place by feeding its soul. I'm privileged to have been associated with the effort, and with the people involved.

Thank you.

JIM HANKLA WAS the city manager when I first came to Long Beach in 1992. A career bureaucrat, he was understandably leery of the new newspaper guy. I, as a newspaper guy, was understandably leery of a big city mover and shaker – and Hankla was nothing if not a mover and shaker.

We developed a relationship based on mutual respect. The Chamber award gave me a good excuse to explain what I found fascinating and worthwhile about Mr. Hankla.

Feb. 7, 2002

According to the American Heritage Dictionary, an entrepreneur is "a person who organizes, operates and assumes the risk for a business venture." Does that describe James Hankla, the CEO of the Alameda Corridor Transportation Authority? Does it describe the Hankla who was Long Beach's city manager for 11 years (from 1987 to 1998)?

The Long Beach Chamber of Commerce thinks so. That group has named Hankla the 2001 Entrepreneur of the Year. The honor, which Chamber President Randy Gordon calls the most prestigious the group offers to individuals, will be presented March 14 at the annual Economic Outlook Conference.

You should know that I serve on the Chamber board – been there for several years. But I had nothing to do with this selection. The full board didn't vote on it.

I agree completely with the choice, though. Hankla is a prototypical entrepreneur. He just happens to do it in the public sector.

The pick was a tad controversial. After all, when people think of entrepreneurs, they think of private business people – those "captains of industry" who make the capitalistic machine move forward.

The Chamber has followed that model with previous awards. There was Diane Creel, the architect of Earth Tech. Next came Chris Pook, creator of the Toyota Grand Prix of Long Beach. Joseph Prevratil, savior of the Queen Mary (among other accomplishments), was the third winner.

Skip Keesal, last year's honoree, didn't exactly fit the accepted mold. But if you are at all aware of his law firm's dealings in the city, the state and the world, you can't see Keesal as anything but an entrepreneur.

But Hankla hasn't owned a business in his life. His short stint in private industry, a couple of years in the early '80s, actually was with outfits whose primary business was with the government.

Perhaps the most common complaint will be that he never put his own money on the line. I feel like I got to know him better than most, at least in a professional way, and I can tell you he felt like he was spending his own money when he dealt with public funds. And part of it was – he was a taxpayer too.

When I think of an entrepreneur, I think of someone who has created something out of nothing – an integrated environmental company, a major car race out of an idea, a successful attraction out of an abandoned hulk of a ship. Hankla also fits that mold.

Whether you agreed with his methods or not -- and there were plenty who didn't – Hankla was one of the most creative public managers I've ever seen when it came to finding ways to get things done. And most of the time, he was able to convince everyone to go along with him.

There were many examples, but just one that comes to mind would have been enough to earn the honor. In the middle of a national recession, and one that hit Long Beach harder than most, Hankla creatively found the financing to more than double the size of the city's Convention Center. That project continues to have a positive impact on the city's economy today.

The list goes on and on – actual construction to comply with the Americans with Disabilities Act, increases in police staffing, keeping the Queen Mary in the city, etc. He did most of that while dealing with a recessionary city budget, the disappearance of the Navy and a state that saw cities as cash cows.

That's an entrepreneur. Good pick, Chamber.

20 YEARS OF SALT

AS EXECUTIVE EDITOR, I felt it was my job to develop close relationships with the city managers, police and fire chiefs and other top officials. Jerry Miller made it easy, with an openness unusual for a top bureaucrat. He took the top spot after several months as the acting city manager, offering a chance to have something to judge the decision by.

May 22, 2003

> For every time, there is a season.
> For every city manager, there has been a time.
> I've been bemused by the reaction of our beloved City Hall critics to the appointment of Jerry Miller as city manager. The lament is that it signals more of the same at City Hall instead of the change promised by the City Council when they summarily dismissed Miller's predecessor, Henry Taboada.
> This particular complaint is proof positive that these people will whine no matter what the facts might be. Hasn't anyone been paying attention to what's gone on at City Hall for the last seven months?
> Miller signaled from virtually the first day he became acting city manager that there would be no more business as usual. He said that in hindsight it was clear city administration and the City Council had mishandled the budget, at least in terms of fiscal responsibility for the long haul. He didn't bemoan the fact that city voters had help put the city in its bad position with approval of a utility tax cut or that it was the state's fault for balancing its budget on cities' backs — he said a problem existed and set out to fix it.
> In a truly unprecedented approach, he and his staff created and pushed a citywide survey to have residents tell government what it is they wanted. More incredible, he not only gave the impression that he was listening to the community, he actually used the survey results to set priorities in his proposed budget.
> Side note: Some people, most notably the losers in the new budget plan, contend that the survey was flawed. I tend to agree,

and further really dislike the notion of government by survey.

But the fact remains, a primary complaint against Taboada and his predecessor, Jim Hankla, was that they did not take the opinions of the "little people" into account.

It's hard to figure out how Miller could have more clearly signaled a change in approach.

Miller is attacked as an insider. Well, toiling for more than 20 years in an attempt to make a city work will do that to you. But the fact is, Miller's familiarity with City Hall's back corridors will allow him to affect change much more quickly than someone who would have to take a year to discover what halls lead where. It's a matter of will, not a matter of tenure.

I should point out that I consider both Henry Taboada and Jim Hankla to be personal friends. Hankla also was one of the most effective city leaders I've ever seen.

Hankla was great then. He would not be a good city manager in Long Beach today. His forte was in connecting the dots, seeing the big picture and forging ahead with a vision. Jim never was very good at making the public a part of the process, or at placating politicos. Both are critical for Long Beach's city manager today.

Taboada got caught as the transition man. He wanted to manage like Hankla, but that time had passed. His creativity in getting things done (a trait Hankla valued when Henry was his assistant) became his undoing. The time had passed.

Miller worked under both Hankla and Taboada. He saw what worked and what didn't. But he also saw how the environment was changing, and how city government had to change with it. He surprised more than a few people with his perceptiveness.

One thing that Miller promised – and this happened long before he actually became a viable option for the full-time job – was that there would be no more business as usual. He got the permanent job by fulfilling that promise.

It's time for a change. It's time to move on.

It's Miller time.

20 YEARS OF SALT

AS A NEWSPAPER editor, you should, I should, expect that I would be all in favor of publishing everything possible. But I have to say that I believe there are lines that aren't necessary to cross.

Another publication in Long Beach decided to take the law opening city payroll records to the public beyond that line. That paper published salaries not only of top management, but all the way down to clerk. Not only that, it put names next to those salaries, not positions.

I took issue with that. I wasn't alone.

Aug. 28, 2003

If I wanted to stir up our little office here, if I wanted to set one person against another, what would I do first?

I'd post a list of salaries on the bulletin board.

I'd make sure one salesperson knew that another salesperson was making a little more than they were. I'd point out to writer A that writer B was making almost as much as they were, even though writer A consistently had more stories in the paper.

About the only thing that defines people's self-worth more than their salaries is their ability to please their lover. Even the most self-effacing team player will feel a twinge of envy – or guilt – if salaries are being compared.

Now if I want to make very sure that every employee in the company hates the management, I'll print their salaries in the newspaper. That way, all their neighbors and friends will either envy or pity them, depending on the size of the salary.

Of course, I will never do either of those things. Our payroll is private, and that includes privacy from each other.

So how, may I ask, is city government any different? Why should I be able to know how much every one of Long Beach's thousands of employees make in a week?

The obvious answer is that they are public employees. Ultimately, they work for me – and you – and we should be able to know how much we're paying for the work to be done.

I should be able to know how much I (the city) am paying the cop on the beat or the guy digging the ditch or the librarian checking out the book. I sure have the right to know how much the city manager makes, or City Council members.

So why is it I felt guilty while I perused the salary list of every manager and administrative assistant in the city in last Sunday's daily newspaper? What was that sort of sick feeling in my stomach? Is this the way Peeping Tom felt?

I know these salaries are public record. I won't get into an argument about whether there are more than 100 employees worth more than $100,000 a year in Long Beach, nor will I argue against publishing the salaries of the city manager, the police chief or any other head honcho.

But does it really make sense to point out that one executive secretary makes $9,000 a year more than the other executive secretary she sits next to every day?

I'll tell you right now that City Prosecutor Tom Reeves doesn't feel good about the fact that it is front page news he makes $35,000 less than fellow lawyer City Attorney Bob Shannon. Still, they are top elected officials, and they know they'll have to deal with their salaries being bandied about.

But does the world really need to know that David Ashman, the new manager of special events, makes $10,000 more than Wilma Powell, the highly regarded director of trade and maritime services at the port? I work with Ashman, and he's worth every penny, but that doesn't make the comparison right.

Discussion of management and employee salaries is an important part of budget discussion, and comparison of positions is a legitimate exercise. But attaching names to numbers is just a divisive, voyeuristic exercise on the level of the National Enquirer.

It was a mean-spirited decision to publish that list. Speaking as a journalist, I'm sorry it happened.

20 YEARS OF SALT

A SCHOOL DISTRICT is the heart and soul of a city. I began covering the Long Beach Unified School District the week I came to town. I got to know the players well, and when they reached the pinnacle of the Broad Prize, I enjoyed celebrating with them.

Sept. 25, 2003

There are more than a few puffed-up chests in Long Beach this week.

That is understandable, since our school district has been named the best in the nation. Even better, the prize goes to those who need it the most – the students. The Broad Foundation's $500,000 will definitely sweeten the college pot for the class of 2004.

Add the $125,000 in scholarships the district received last year for being a finalist, and Eli Broad has definitely done good by Long Beach (even if he wouldn't like that sentence).

I have to say that the award seemed a slam-dunk to me. I don't know the story of every urban school district in the country, but it is hard to picture one more innovative – or more caring – than Long Beach. And I'd like to invoke the name of the late, great Ed Eveland to explain.

Eveland was a believer in tough love before it was a pop psychology phrase. As principal at Wilson High, then as a school board member, he showed students he cared by giving them the tools to succeed – and forcing them to use those tools.

Eveland was a prime supporter of then-superintendent Carl Cohn's efforts to return discipline and high expectations to Long Beach schools. There's a reason the whole school uniform craze began in east Long Beach, which Eveland represented.

Eveland, Cohn and current Superintendent Chris Steinhauser were way ahead of the curve when it came to demanding that students reach minimum achievement levels before moving up the school ladder. (I'll have to admit, I never understood how students with "Fs" moved on to the next grade in the first place, but I come from an older time.) Long Beach was forcing fifth graders to read and eighth graders to write and do 'rithmetic long before the state decided a test was required to make a high school diploma mean something.

More impressively, Steinhauser's administration has managed to keep improving the academics and balance the budget in very tough money times. I think it goes back to another Eveland philosophy – get the basics done first, and do them well. The rest will follow.

I've experienced how it works firsthand. My stepson, John, just started high school. He chose to go to Cabrillo, the new school on the west side. (Who ever heard of getting to choose your high school?)

Put simply, Cabrillo is urban high school died and gone to heaven. The student mix is culturally diverse and economically challenged. Yet the campus is state-of-the-art and the curriculum keeps the individual student in mind. They give every student every chance to succeed.

I was privileged to receive my early education in what was then considered one of the top suburban school districts in the country – Jefferson County School District in Colorado. I'm privileged now to send John to the top urban school district in the country.

My chest is swelling.

Congratulations, Long Beach. Job well done.

THE SALE OF Gazette Newspapers to the same corporation that owned the Long Beach Press-Telegram and the Los Angeles Daily News undoubtedly was a bigger deal for those of us employed at the paper than it was to the community at large. That remained the case, at least for the first five years or so, thanks to a promise exacted by the Blowitzes from Media News to keep the papers separate and competitive.

As the Internet and social media accelerated the rate of change in the media world, the Gazette was afforded the chance to see how the community newspaper philosophy fit into that new environment. It continues to be a challenge – change in progress.

Jan. 8, 2004

Change. Do you know anyone who likes it? I don't.
Change is uncomfortable. Change is hard work. Change is, well, change.
Change also is the definition of life. If you're not changing, you're dead. Stagnant. Inert. No change is, well, unchanging.
Our loyal readers know that we at the Gazette have believed in change. Not change for change's sake, but change for improvement. I would like to humbly submit that we have met that challenge. We are alive, better than we were in the past and a vital part of the community.
Now we are facing another change. I'll not lie to you (I never have) – we're a tad nervous about the unknown. We wouldn't be human if we weren't.
But my history here has given me confidence that we will emerge from this change better, and able to do a better job for you. That's not just my Pollyanna side talking, either. It's based on my personal experience at the Gazette in Long Beach, and what little I know about what the future holds.
Let me start with what I know about – the past. When I first walked into the Gazette offices nearly 12 years ago, I was walking

away from a career in daily newspapers and back to my roots in community newspapering.

I made the move because of two people – Fran and John Blowitz. Wait, that's not quite right. I made the move because those two people had the same philosophy I did about what a newspaper can and should be to its community.

We built from what they had started. We were blessed with a great nucleus for a team, and were lucky enough to find the right players to add as we went along. Every year, when we sat down to discuss what had happened, we were able to say, "This is the best bunch of people we've ever had." That's still true today.

There were tough times, for sure. That goes for personal tough times as well as professional tough times. But John and Fran were always there for me when I needed them, and I like to think I was there for them when they needed me.

We changed. We grew.

That attitude extends throughout the Gazette. We have been, and still are, a family. We are a family that calls Long Beach home.

It's going to be different not having John and Fran around. Not better, hopefully not worse, but different. It's going to be a change.

It's going to be a change working with new people at the Los Angeles Newspaper Group and MediaNews Inc. Hopefully, it's going to be a change we see, but you don't notice too much.

Because one thing I don't expect to change is the ability to put out a quality newspaper for our community. And I don't expect to change my reliance on the great people here. And my friendship and respect for Fran and John will not change.

That's one of the great things about life – you can change while still keeping some things the same. That's change for the better, not change for the sake of change.

Change is around the corner. I'll see you there.

20 YEARS OF SALT

THE COLLISION BETWEEN dwindling city resources and increasing crime, specifically gang crime, began to have impacts in 2004 – the Parks and Recreation gang intervention unit mentioned below was eliminated later that year. I tried to put a personal face on the issue with this column.

Jan. 22, 2004

I put together one of those home gyms last weekend. (My wife keeps getting me this exercise stuff, for some reason. But that's another column.)

You've seen these things – they have about 750,000 pieces, with cables stretching every which way. They're able to work every part of your body.

And that's just while you're trying to put it together.

I used every tool I could find – including 14-year-old stepson John – to put the thing together. John saved me more than one miscue, and having the right tools allowed us to successfully complete the project in one afternoon.

While we were doing it, I thought more than once about Long Beach's current push to ease the gang violence problem. A stretch? Not really. In the first place, John was in the garage, working with me, instead of running the streets (which, thank God, he shows little inclination to do).

Second, I thought about the tools we were using to do the job. Sure, we used some big wrenches and I even brought the hammer out once. But we also used a delicate allen wrench and, perhaps more importantly, some thought and planning.

I want to urge that we take the same approach as we fight to stop gang violence. I'm all in favor of the efforts made by Chief Tony Batts and his police department to bring the hammer down on the gangs. I support Prosecutor Tom Reeves' gang injunction approach to taking back the streets.

I'm particularly impressed with the efforts of Al Bernstein and the Office of Intervention and Prevention Services. That's a quiet little outfit in the Department of Parks, Recreation and Marine that has evolved from the gang intervention program. He does everything from tattoo removal to setting up peace talks between rival gangs.

But, as we go into what will undoubtedly be the most painful city budget process seen in Long Beach in decades, we have to remember not to throw out all the little tools we need to do the job of preventing gang violence. We have to resist the strident cries for more cops to the exclusion of all else and look at the longer term even as we try to stem the current flow of blood.

Consider this. If there were no members, there would be no gangs. If there were no gangs, there would be no gang violence.

That is the reason Bernstein's office has the word prevention in it. But Bernstein needs tools to keep kids out of gangs. And those tools seldom are in the hands of police officers.

Gang prevention is implicit in recreation programs for youth. Gang alternatives are a primary definition of art programs for youth. Gang turf can be replaced only by libraries and after-school programs.

We have to stop the bleeding, and that will require application of significant pressure. But we also need to solve the underlying disease, and that requires resources for the prevention effort.

It will take a calm, balanced hand to use all the available tools to save our youth. It will take dedication and long-term commitment, just like any fitness program.

The result will be a healthier community. Let the exercise begin.

20 YEARS OF SALT

I HAVE SELDOM been shy about using the Pinch to express opinions about issues I was directly involved in. It was, and is, the only place in the paper I felt comfortable letting myself go – an old-fashioned notion that news should at least attempt to be unbiased.

The sports park issue had it all for me – Parks and Recreation, intractable environmental extremists and a long, long path to an attempted conclusion. I would be less than fair to not point out that we ultimately lost this fight – but to fiscal realities, not environmental blockages.

March 30, 2006

When I first began sharing this space a couple of years ago with outside columnists, the idea was to offer a range of ideas, to stir up some passion.

Little did I know it would be my passion that would be stirred.

Anne-Marie Otey has been writing for the Gazette in one capacity or another for a number of years. Her column, "The Stroller," has been a positive addition to our Commentary page.

But she was way off base last week when she trashed a proposal to create a sports park on what is now the industrial dump sometimes known as Exxon Hill. And not just because she disagreed with me, either.

Otey opined that the entire 55 acres would best be used to create some sort of Ansel Adams portrait of natural days gone by. Her concluding phrase was, and I quote, "We've succeeded in making a park for dogs. Let's do at least as well by humans."

I couldn't agree more. The problem is in the definition of humans.

Apparently, some folks believe that the only humans parks should be made for are those who wish to wander quietly alone, communing with nature. Somehow, those folks who go in for noisy things like soccer or softball (or, heaven forbid, skateboards) don't quite qualify as human.

I too read Emerson, Frost and Thoreau. I lived in the Rocky Mountains, and for a time had my own little Walden Pond (called the Rio Grande).

But I also played baseball and softball. More importantly, I had kids who played baseball, soccer and lots of other noisy games.

The whole "Give me nature or give me death" movement strikes me as hugely one-sided and ultimately extremely elitist. If I could, I'd give everyone their own Walden Pond. But I'd also give sports facilities to those who take their recreation more actively.

But wait – isn't that exactly what the City Council will be asked to take up at Tuesday's study session? It is, indeed.

The latest revision to the sports park includes more than 10 acres – 20% of the available land – for natural habitat and wetlands. Instead of flattening the hill to make the best possible use of the property in a sports fields sense, a high vantage point will remain and access will be created even for the handicapped (it is fenced-off property now, although that hasn't stopped "environmentalists" from visiting frequently to figure out ways to "protect" it).

In other words, the interests of all sides were taken into account. Full disclosure – as a Parks and Recreation Commission member, I was loathe to consider cutting back on fields to placate what I believe to be a small but vocal minority. But those nasty folks known as city staff finally convinced me that this actually was a better project than what we had started with exactly because all sides had been heard.

Be aware that the City Council could, and might, go back to the original all-sports plan. Passions have been stirred.

I hope that I have at least attempted to look at both sides before letting my passion leak onto the page.

20 YEARS OF SALT

THIS IS THE easiest column in this book to justify. It was one of the hardest to write.

A 12-year stint of leading the city is just the tip of the iceberg when it comes to Beverly O'Neill. That's why I wrote a book about her. It also is why it was so hard to cram what I wanted to say in one short column. But here's what resulted.

June 1, 2006

When Beverly O'Neill picks up the phone, I invariably respond with the same greeting:

"How's my favorite mayor today?"

It's a bit of an inside joke — O'Neill is my only mayor, and has been for the last 12 years. But it's also true — she has won my heart.

People started thanking Beverly six months ago, so I don't think this column is too early, even though she will be mayor for another six weeks or so. I'm using my executive privilege to scoop myself as well — our tribute to "The O'Neill Years" will appear in next week's paper.

I'm doing it to get a few observations in early enough to be seen as at least semi-original, before everyone else says them. So eat my dust, all you sycophants.

When Beverly first ran for office in 1994, I openly questioned her qualifications. She was an educator, after all, not a politician. She was one of 13 candidates; almost an afterthought when looking at a field that included the incumbent mayor, two City Council members and the head of the powerful Redevelopment Agency board.

The election result is one reason I no longer prognosticate these things. Bev smoked the field in the primary, then trounced one of the better one-on-one politicians I know, Ray Grabinski.

Next, I challenged Her Honor for not taking stands on every issue coming down the pike. I will forever live with the shame of being one of the first to call her "just a cheerleader."

Dr. O'Neill educated me early on. I watched as she convinced a city of more than 400,000 that they could indeed survive after the Navy had gone. I wondered as she convinced a federal government leery of helping anyone do anything to provide concrete (literally) help to remake Long Beach into something viable.

I was left amazed as she guided a cantankerous, often pettily self-centered group of council members to a common vision for the city's future. The cheerleader stood quietly as others cheered.

Five years ago, I was ready to sanctify the ever-positive Saint Bev and see her move on. When I told her I didn't want to see her run as a write-in candidate, it honestly was because I didn't want to see her get hurt by the fickle and heartless electorate.

The professor schooled me again. She said she had more work to do, and convinced the voters she could do it. Her unprecedented write-in victory has been chronicled nationally, so I don't need to do it at length again here.

She sure taught me not to underestimate the power of positive thinking (and doing), though.

O'Neill began her last four years as mayor much as she did her first four – staring at a demoralized city with huge budget problems, and wondering how she could make it better. She did it the same way, as well – bringing people together and convincing them to work in the same direction.

All respect to Frank Colonna and Bob Foster, but I think Long Beach would be better off if Beverly were mayor for four more years. I'm glad she's stepping down, though. I don't think Beverly would be better off if Beverly were mayor for four more years.

That matters to me, because she is my favorite mayor, after all. And she always will be.

FULL DISCLOSURE HERE – I've become personal friends with Jerry Miller. We have quite a bit in common, although he is a better golfer than I am – a fault I decided to overlook. More important were two passions we shared – Long Beach and Beverly O'Neill. We worked for their welfare, me in the periphery, him in the center of the action.

Here's my take on the end of his public career.

May 31, 2007

Jerry Miller might not be a man for all seasons, but he certainly was a man for this season.

I first met Miller when he was manager of the Economic Development Bureau – not an enviable job in the early 1990s, let me assure you. But then City Manager Jim Hankla knew what he was doing by putting Miller there. The man is a can-do sort of guy.

I have to admit, I thought Miller was pretty good at that job, but didn't really understand what was going on when Hankla brought him up to the 13th floor as a deputy city manager. I didn't really find out why, either – Miller stayed in the background.

It made more sense when Henry Taboada tapped Jerry as the assistant city manager. Taboada (who I consider a personal friend) felt the need for the spotlight, and required a quiet second in command.

When Miller was thrust into the top spot after the coup that unseated Taboada, I was among the doubters. I simply didn't know the man that well, and questioned whether he had the personality, vision and skill needed to lead the city out of what had become a quagmire of financial trouble and public mistrust.

Boy, was I wrong.

Miller confronted the budget issues squarely, making elimination of a nine-figure general fund deficit not just the top priority, but the only priority. More telling was the way he did it.

He asked the community to participate in a survey prioritizing city services. Then, in an unprecedented early public discussion of the budget, he and his staff used those survey results to justify the necessary service cuts to get the budget back into balance.

If there is one thing that carries more weight with City Council members than their own desires, it is the expressed desire of the people who elect them. Miller managed to hand the council a plan that they could not reject without looking like they were rejecting the will of the voters.

Just as importantly, Miller's approach gave the public, at least the part of the public that cared, a feeling of ownership. In the popular jargon of the day, even the critics had to admit to a certain amount of buy-in.

That masterpiece of management handed Miller the city manager's job. Then it was up to him to prove it wasn't a fluke. That's exactly what he did.

Miller adheres to the management philosophy of hiring good people and getting out of the way. In less than five years, he has replaced department heads in all but two of the city's primary departments under the city manager's control (directors at the Harbor and Water departments are hired by independent commissions). It says something that the two department heads remaining, Ron Arias at Health and Human Services and Phil Hester at Parks, Recreation and Marine, are both acknowledged as among the best in their fields.

Miller hired talent, regardless of perceived drawbacks. His picks for police chief and fire chief both were the youngest appointed in recent memory. Both Anthony Batts and David Ellis are now stars in their own rights.

He tapped Chris Shippey as the city's first female assistant city manager. She's now the city's first female acting city manager and has a good chance to become the city's first female city manager.

Miller plucked Suzanne Mason out of the ranks to become his budget guru. She's now director of Human Resources. He hired women to become department heads at both Public Works and Planning and Building – traditional male bailiwicks, to be sure.

The list goes on and on. I'm proud to call Mr. Miller Jerry these days, and proud to say he proved me wrong.

He was, indeed, the man for this season.

I MAKE NO apologies for believing that Joe Prevratil consistently did what he believed was best for the city. I know he did what he believed was best for the people around him. I watched him try for more than a decade to keep Long Beach's icon, the Queen Mary, a viable concern.

Full disclosure, I had the honor of being married by Captain Prevratil aboard his ship. The day they made him walk away from that ship was a sad one indeed.

Aug. 16, 2007

How quickly we forget.

Listen to some people at City Hall these days or read some self-proclaimed "news sources," and you'd be certain that Joe Prevratil is the devil incarnate. According to these Pharisees, the man is out to suck the city dry through the straw of the Queen Mary.

Bull.

As I write this, lawyers and developers are filing into a court-room to bid on the assets of Queen's Seaport Development Inc., Prevratil's for-profit business formed to develop the land around the landmark Queen Mary. That is separate and distinct from the nonprofit RMS Foundation, which has the sublease to operate the ship itself.

By the end of the year, Prevratil will vacate the office on the Sun Deck that he has maintained for the last 14 years. The 70-year-old is set to retire. He feels, correctly, that some in the city can't wait to see him go.

A sad state of affairs.

Flash back to 1992. The powerhouse Disney Company had abandoned ship, sore at the city's apparent inability to sway the state into granting approval for a Disney By The Sea. The Harbor Commission, tired of dealing with a ship that didn't move, appeared poised to sell the Queen to the highest bidder and allow them to tow it away.

City officials, including then-City Manager James Hankla and then-City Councilman Jeff Kellogg, opined that Long Beach couldn't lose its identifying icon. The council "bought" responsibility for the ship back from the Port of Long Beach, and waited for a knight in shining armor.

In rode Prevratil. He received standing ovations at both Harbor Commission and City Council meetings. He saved the Queen.

Don't believe it? Talk to the 500 or so employees who have had steady jobs on the ship. Talk to attendees of the annual Scottish Festival, Shipwreck, New Year's Eve or any of the other major special events based on the ship.

Prevratil started with a five-year lease, then took it to a 20-year lease, then one for 66 years. Each time, council members praised his vision and commitment to the city.

I watched as he juggled options, floated trial balloons and crafted alliances in attempts to not just keep the Queen afloat, but make it a viable operation. In fact, before the Sept. 11, 2001, terrorist attacks leveled the tourism business just as completely as it leveled the Twin Towers, Prevratil actually had the ship operations in the black for a year or two.

A city in a severe budget crunch began to squeeze the Queen Mary operation just as Prevratil found himself essentially back to square one in trying to create a viable enterprise across the bay. When Prevratil fought back, acrimony began to ooze between the squeezing fingers.

The legal and business machinations that followed could fill a book. I've written a fair chunk of it myself – and I'm still not willing to say one side or the other has right on its side.

What I am willing to say is that Joe Prevratil is no devil.

Just follow him around the ship some day and watch how the crew reacts to his presence. Better, talk to the many longtime employees outside of his presence.

The man is revered. That's no exaggeration, either.

Joe was one of the first true movers and shakers I met when I came to town more than 15 years ago. At the time he had been entrusted with the expansion of the Convention Center, and our first meeting had something to do with excavation of part of the old Rainbow Pier. He was worrying about what to do and still move the project forward.

Since then, he has become a friend – a good friend. Yet he never attempted to use that friendship to sway coverage of his endeavors, and understood when I tried to set the friendship aside to do my job.

I admire and respect both his abilities and his character. He's no saint, but he's a lot closer to that end of the scale than being a devil.

Joe Prevratil will have a legacy in Long Beach, and in my book it will be a shining one. He's done many things, but most of all, he saved the Queen.

Remember that.

TASK FORCES AND studies are part of the way American democracy does business. I have had the pleasure, or the misfortune, to participate in the process several times in Long Beach. Once the study is done, the hard part begins – selling the plan.

This was yet another attempt by me to do that. It didn't work, largely due to circumstance, but I think the argument is still worthwhile.

April 1, 2009

Every planning process I've been involved in – and I've been involved in a few – has been lengthy, frustrating and ultimately ending in a less-than-satisfying result.

Yet every one of those plans was worthwhile, and made a difference in our city.

The current effort to create a new Cultural Plan for Long Beach is a perfect example. I joined 74 of my closest friends to be part of a steering committee for this effort, which is co-coordinated by the city's infant Cultural Affairs Bureau and the Arts Council for Long Beach. Money for the bare-bones budget comes from the Los Angeles Arts Council.

There's a bit of deja vu involved in the discussions for this plan. I was part of a similar process more than a decade ago, culminating in the first Long Beach Cultural Arts Plan in 1996. Since then, I've led two separate full-blown studies on funding for the arts.

Sadly, the timing for both the funding studies was about as bad as it could be, and both were shelved. But the cultural plan and its companion financial impact report did have a large and positive impact, both at the government and the private levels.

It raised the profile of the arts in Long Beach to unprecedented levels. During the few flush years the government experienced at the turn of the century, the plan was the ammunition that won increased funding from the city. Even the public art program became self-sufficient.

Unfortunately, support for the arts declined right along with – and sometimes in advance of – support for all sorts of "amenities." That was true both on a government and a private level. Like it or not, money for the arts is usually the first thing to go when budgets – public or private – get tight.

Which is exactly the reason why it makes so much sense to complete a new cultural plan now. As President Obama and his advisors like to say, this economic crisis is too good to waste.

The winners coming out of this recession are going to be those who have planned in advance. If the artists and arts organizations of Long Beach want to improve their situation when the general situation improves, they better have a strategy.

And it's time to go through the entire process again. While there are some old salts (pun intended) like me still around, the vast majority of the players have changed. Certainly the leaders – Justin Hectus at the Arts Council, Antonio Ruiz at the Creativity Network, Robert Swayze at the Cultural Affairs Bureau – are all new to the scene. So are many of the individual artists and leaders of arts organizations and institutions.

And it's time to once again reinforce the importance of the arts and culture for our city's well being. An engagement with some aspect of art and culture – from looking at a picture to visiting a rancho, from dancing a jig to listening to the symphony – is the very definition of quality of life.

Cultural education is feeding the soul of our community's children. Numerous studies have shown that involvement with the arts translates to higher educational achievement, and it's clear that a teenager involved in music, performing or visual arts is less likely to become involved in gangs.

That message, when hard budget decisions are being made, has to be heard. And one of the best ways to get it heard is to involve the community in a process to weave arts and culture into the fabric of Long Beach life.

I've typically said at the end of these planning exercises that

I never wanted to go through another one. I'm glad I'm going through this one, even on the periphery. It is indeed important to our city's future.

That means it's important to me.

OVER THE YEARS, I've often used a blip in the news cycle to peg a column on. More often than not, I've had an ulterior motive, or at least a larger topic to explore.

That approach worked even better than I expected when Long Beach's Library Foundation chose "The Soloist" as its 2010 Long Beach Reads One Book selection.

March 10, 2010

For the last week or so, Long Beach has been reading one book – "The Soloist," by Los Angeles Times columnist Steve Lopez.

It's got a really long subtitle: "A Lost Dream, An Unlikely Friendship And The Redemptive Power of Music." But unless you actually are one of those who has read the book (or seen the movie), you probably aren't aware that the book's subject is both homeless and mentally ill.

It is an amazing tale, and what the critics call an "unflinching look" at the reality of mental illness, homelessness and the connection between the two. Long Beach has its own fair share of disturbed homeless people, but none of them have attended Julliard.

At least we don't know that they have. Homeless people are notoriously reticent when it comes to talking to members of the press – in fact, that's one reason Lopez's book is such a triumph.

I have a vested interest in solving, or at least alleviating, the problem of homeless people in Long Beach. As a paper, we've spotlighted the problem at least twice in the last decade. I served on the steering committee for something called the Ten-Year Plan To End Homelessness a couple of years back, and actually wrote the foreword for that report.

The City Council finally accepted the report a couple months ago. Fortunately, the dedicated staff in the city's Health and Human Resources Department (led by Susan Price) already has worked hard to implement many of the plan's proposals.

My involvement in the process was a great education – as, it is clear in his book, Lopez's involvement with Nathaniel Ayers was. Perhaps the most important thing I learned was that, while they are by far the most visible, the lone homeless street people are far from the only type of homeless people in our city. In fact, the public rarely sees the majority of the homeless, who often are families or women with children.

I also learned that Long Beach is at the cutting edge of helping serve the homeless population and alleviate the problems they face. The Villages at Cabrillo and the Multi-Service Center there provide a one-stop shop for those trying to climb out of the pit of homelessness. The Mary Bethune School there is a prototype others across the country copy as it prepares homeless children to transition back to the school system.

There's even a Christ-based preschool for homeless children called Precious Lamb. I didn't learn about that one while I was working on the Ten-Year Plan. I'm on Precious Lamb's board, and would be pleased to tell you about it if you like. But we'll do that one-on-one. Give me a call.

Back to the city. The Mental Health Association (MHA) facility in Long Beach, called the Village, deals with the mental health problems of the homeless people. That's where Lopez went for more understanding, and where a lot of good work is being done.

But one of the sad things I learned, and kind of the moral of Lopez's story as I read it, is that not everyone wants to be "saved" from homelessness. We can say that fierce desire to stay unfettered and on the street is a sign of mental illness, and in most cases that truly is a factor, but the fact remains, if someone doesn't want to change their situation, there's little anyone can do to change it.

The same is true for addictive behavior – alcoholism, drug dependence, gambling, etc. Recognition of the problem is the first step in solving the problem, and for some homeless people, there simply isn't a problem.

Should we continue to try to help? Lopez did. Many others in Long Beach do.

Because, but for the grace of God, there go I. That's the real lesson, and one well worth learning.

20 YEARS OF SALT

OCCASIONALLY, AN IMPORTANT citywide issue coincides with a compelling individual issue. When it happens, I try to connect the dots to come up with a column. The connection between seamless education and Doug Otto held a lot of meaning to me.

March 24, 2011

> I was dragging Monday morning.
> Not physically — Sunday's rain kept me inside. But mentally and emotionally, I was pretty drained.
> Part of it was the ongoing tragedy in Japan. How can you live in Southern California and not both empathize and worry when we're talking earthquake (the Big One, for sure), tsunami and nuclear danger?
> Part of it was the insanity in the Arab world, particularly in Libya. The actions of a lunatic like Gaddafi cause me to despair that there ever will be sanity, let alone peace, in this world.
> A big part of it was the airplane crash last Wednesday. I knew these men, considered Mark Bixby in particular a friend. All were younger than I am, still going through that incredible life experience called raising children. Sorry and sympathy aren't adequate words to convey the feelings.
> So it was really, really important for me to attend the Long Beach College Promise event on Monday morning. If you aren't aware of it by now, the promise is the culmination of the Seamless Education approach Long Beach has been pioneering for more than a decade. Students can literally go from kindergarten to an advanced college degree now without ever leaving Long Beach, thanks to the promise.
> What promise? A promise of a free semester at Long Beach City College after graduating from the Long Beach Unified School District. A promise of placement preference at California State University, Long Beach, with qualifying grades.

In short, it is a promise of support for children willing to make the effort to get an education.

Monday morning, a student from every middle school and K-8 school in Long Beach received a certificate emblematic of that promise to get them ready for college and into college. Most of those youngsters had a bit of the deer-in-the-headlights look as they stood in front of the college presidents and the school district superintendent for the obligatory photo.

But those students represented Long Beach's, our country's, our world's future. And the event represented an attempt by talented, caring adults to make sure that future is bright.

I needed that.

But I got a bonus on Monday morning – a big bonus.

His name is Doug Otto. Some of you might know him as an attorney in town. Some might remember he was on the city's Planning Commission. Others might have voted for him to serve on the Long Beach City College Board of Trustees.

He is, as they say, a mover and shaker in Long Beach; a person to be reckoned with and a person to go to when you want something done. He is my friend.

He also is a cancer survivor.

Last June, Doug was diagnosed with cancer of the neck. He had tumors in his neck and at the base of his tongue. The prognosis wasn't good – but then cancer prognosis and good seem to me to be mutually-exclusive terms.

For some time, Doug's illness was no more than a whisper among friends. Then, thorough tactician that he is, Doug and his wife Freda came up with a battle plan. And that plan included a way to let friends keep up to date through a web-based journal. His arduous fight against cancer became a public battle, with many of us cheering from the sidelines.

Monday was Doug's coming-out party of sorts. He sat in the front row with the rest of the trustees to watch a program he had helped craft and support.

We talked. We hugged. He's more soft-spoken now, but he spoke. He is back. He is alive.

That affirmation lifted my heart on a day it needed lifting.

I continue to ponder the mystery of why one person is taken and another is saved. I confess I do not understand, and have no answer when I am asked how God can allow things to take place that seem unfair, downright cruel.

But I know there is good in the world as well as tragedy, hope as well as sorrow. Monday gave me that.

I pray that somehow, I might give a little of it to you.

Part FIVE
The Spirit Of Faith

THE SPIRIT OF FAITH

LONG BEACH HAS had a large and vibrant gay and lesbian community for decades, and the city has been in the forefront of tolerance efforts pretty much since the beginning. But it was far from a unanimous feeling. And when gays were attacked verbally, they attacked right back.

The Gazette – and I – was in the middle. I tried to calm the debate with this statement of social reality. Sadly, it didn't work. I put a moratorium on gay issue-related letters a month later.

Feb. 18, 1993

A storm is brewing.

It's been building for more than two months now. One letter fires accusations of a group being a "societal problem," the next charges bigotry, the next, hatred.

Recently, the debate in the Grunion's "We Get Letters" column has heated up – heated to the point where it's time to do a little cooling off. That's not because of the phone calls I've been getting – from both sides, I might add – but because the rhetoric is reaching beyond the reality.

Gays and lesbians are a fact of life in this world – even more-so here in Southern California than in many places. They have fought, just as ethnic minorities have fought, for the right to pursue happiness on an equal footing.

It's also a fact that there remains a large conservative element in the Long Beach population – Iowa by the Sea remains a fact for many. And a large share of those people grew up being taught that homosexual behavior was an aberration.

So it comes as no surprise that the two groups clash. Add in the righteous indignation of one side for being discriminated against, and the belief on the other side that morality is being assailed, and the passionate tone of the arguments become understandable.

But it's time for some tolerance here.

The argument that gays and lesbians are responsible for a disproportionate share of society's troubles doesn't hold water. In fact, we who live so closely with the gay community should be more aware than most that they run clean businesses and care for their homes and neighborhoods as well as, if not better than, any other segment of society.

There remains a perception that the deadly AIDS virus is somehow the responsibility of the gay community. I suspect that is a holdover from the same mindset that considered syphilis, gonorrhea and any other sexually transmitted disease to be just punishment for "immoral" behavior.

Two points here. First, the reality is, AIDS is transmitted in other ways besides unprotected sex – shared needles and bad blood transfusions, just to name two. And while the disease has hit the homosexual community particularly hard, they certainly don't have a patent on promiscuity – check the teen-age pregnancy figures.

Second, what happened to compassion? Would you deny care and concern to a neighbor whose smoking led to incurable lung cancer?

We at Gazette Newspapers believe the homosexual community is a vital and valuable part of Long Beach. We support their right to pursue happiness without the anchor of discrimination.

Which does not mean that we will not print letters of the opposite point of view. Our letters section functions as a place for community debate, and to limit one side of that debate defeats the purpose.

I contend that we have to stare irrational prejudice in the face in order to combat that prejudice. If you refuse to acknowledge an enemy, it is impossible to defeat that enemy.

That does not, however, mean the debate should be allowed to become inflammatory, I dislike editing letters to the editor – the whole point is to allow people to express their opinions in their own words. And you can help.

Think before you write. Take a moment to ask yourself if you are adding to the debate with a reasoned comment, or just fanning the flames.

Then let your opinion be known.

I'M A WORD guy, and I'm more aware than most that words can hurt. But I also have very little patience with political correctness, particularly when it seems overly sensitive and misdirected.

In this case, I tried to respond with restraint and respect. Really I did.

June 6, 1996

> There's nothing like a little controversy to get the blood moving. If you don't think so, check out Our Mailbox this week.
> Normally we publish letters from our readers without comment. After all, the whole point of a letters column is to allow people to express their opinions without censorship.
> But this week, I'm compelled to exercise my prerogative as the person in control of this space. Letter writers John Scanlon and Raymond Sheelen raise issues that deserve a reply, and cannot be addressed in a one-sentence editor's note.
> It all started last week, with a letter from Patrick McAnish, which characterized the Gazette as "a complete Fag Rag." The letter apparently was in response to a special section published May 16 spotlighting the annual Lesbian and Gay Pride Festival.
> Scanlon and Sheelen take me to task for allowing the word "fag" to appear in the newspaper. "I should think it would occur to you that this letter would upset us unnecessarily," Scanlon writes.
> Well, of course I expected people to be upset. And if I had felt McAnish had been denigrating a segment of the community or an individual with name calling, I would have had second thoughts about allowing the letter to appear.
> But the fact is, I considered his comment a slur against the newspaper. In that light, I had no problem with allowing his opinion to be aired. I'll stand by this newspaper's consistent policy to present all sides of the Long Beach community objectively. A little name-calling isn't going to keep us from doing that job.
> There are other reasons to run that type of letter. Like it or not,

McAnish's views represent a segment of society. Acting as if that view doesn't exist would be as much an abdication of our responsibility as following his preferences – ignoring the Lesbian and Gay Pride Festival – would have been.

Here's a little unsolicited advice: The enemy unknown is 10 times as dangerous as the enemy known.

Regarding Scanlon's threat to organize a boycott and Sheelen's promise to "toss it," I guess they are extremely selective readers. Rather than pay any attention to the coverage provided to gay and lesbian issues (not just the week prior to the festival, but on an ongoing basis) or to take note of Publisher John Blowitz's column about tolerance and the justice in the Supreme Court overturning Colorado's anti-homosexual actions just the week before McAnish's letter, these gentlemen opted to focus on one word.

Sheelen and Scanlon question whether I would have made the same decision if the letter had been attacking other minority groups. Again, I say it would depend on the context of the comment. But I also say (again) that ignoring a point of view will not make it go away.

Finally, Scanlon makes reference to a time when I "pulled the plug" on the pro/anti gay debate in the letters. In fact, that occurred two years ago, after nearly two months of back and forth. That decision was made when the "debate" degenerated into name calling between a few rabid writers from both sides. I would, and will, take the same action again if something similar occurs on this or any other issue.

I appreciate the fact people care enough about the Gazette to use it to express their opinions. I hope they appreciate the Gazette being there to allow those opinions to be expressed. I plan to keep it that way.

Now, isn't your blood moving?

THE METAPHOR OF the pendulum to describe various aspects of society has been one of my favorite tools. History bears me out, and I am far from the only one to see its efficacy.

Here is my ode to the pendulum.

July 5, 2001

Consider the common pendulum. One of the closest things we have to a perpetual motion machine, it swings to and fro, passing the center, but stopping there only when it has stopped.

That pendulum is my favorite metaphor to describe the way things work in our society. Going from one extreme to the other, back and forth, back and forth.

It works as a description of the economy. On one end is the boom, heady days of prosperity as production soars, everyone has a job and salaries (and prices) rise. On the other end is the depression, when there is no production because no one has the job or money to buy anything.

Alan Greenspan and the rest of his brethren spend their lives trying to push the pendulum into the middle. Too much boom, they say, and inflation is sure to follow. Too much depression is, well, depressing.

But the worst thing that could happen is for the pendulum to stop. That's the definition of a non-economy.

My magnificent metaphor works even better when it comes to public policy. Okay, we'll use the nasty word – politics. The pendulum swings from conservative to liberal, from Republican to Democrat.

That's not necessarily a bad thing. It takes new ideas, new approaches, to keep the pendulum moving. American voters are notorious for their "throw the bums out" mentality (something that's reaching the extreme end of the pendulum itself); a fact that almost negates the advantage of incumbency these days.

I suspect that people vote against incumbents just to shake

things up as often as they vote that way because they don't like the person in office.

My pendulum postulate reaches near perfection when we look at the broader definition of public policy. Take development in Long Beach, for example. For years, the mantra was development at all costs – give us the jobs, the tax base that was so sorely lacking.

But the pendulum swung. Environmental activists, neighborhood activists and just plain concerned citizens now want development to jump through myriad hoops to make sure their particular interest is fulfilled. Then they are as likely to block the development anyway as not.

These self-appointed watchdogs serve a good purpose. They tug the pendulum back from the developer extreme of profit above all, and usually help arrive at a project that is better in the end.

But they also have the potential to hold the pendulum at their own extreme, which typically comes down to no development at all. That's just as dangerous, maybe more so, than unchecked development.

Finally, there's one more thing about the pendulum metaphor that I love. As the pendulum swings, it hits center twice for every single time it hits one of the extremes.

That's balance. That's what keeps us – and the pendulum – going.

20 YEARS OF SALT

I, LIKE MOST of American society, have found myself evolving in my feelings about homosexual relationships, particularly in terms of gay marriage. This particular column was more about the right of individuals to live in the way they want, not the definition of marriage.

It should be noted that this was more than a decade ago, and even commitment ceremonies were considered controversial.

August 16, 2001

I received a press release last week, actually two press releases, announcing that the wedding chapel aboard the Queen Mary would now offer "commitment ceremonies" to same-sex couples. I wondered why.

Not why the Queen Mary was offering the service, but why it should be considered news. I thought we had made it past that particular hurdle.

As far as I'm concerned, any two people who want to make a commitment to each other should be allowed to do so. The last time I checked, I wasn't a part of that commitment, so why should it matter to me?

And any facility, be it a wedding chapel or a church, should have the right to host whatever ceremonies they want. For the most part, they also should have the right to not host events they do not want to host.

It's called tolerance. When people decide to do something with their personal lives, and that action does not impact my life or beliefs, I simply don't see where I should become involved.

Conservative churches, like mine, will never host a same-sex "commitment" ceremony. But that certainly should not preclude those ceremonies from taking place at all. I might like to convince you of the efficacy of my beliefs, but I'm certainly not interested in imposing them on you.

So why is this new policy aboard the Queen Mary considered news?

Unfortunately, we as a society need to continue to make strides in promoting tolerance and inclusiveness. That makes it news.

Our vice mayor, Dan Baker, is proudly and openly gay, and helped promote the change in policy. That makes it news — especially since Baker is running for mayor.

This, by the way, is the only instance I can recall where Baker has made sexual preference an issue. He downplayed his orientation during his campaign for the Second District council seat. There have been no overt attempts to promote the "gay cause" during his tenure, with Baker's emphasis being instead on efforts to represent all of his constituents.

Baker has said that he believes, as I do, that a person's sexual preference is a personal matter. He has said, as I believe, that a person's sexual preference should not figure in an evaluation of that person's job performance. He has said, as I believe, that sexual preference rarely has anything to do with a person's stand on public issues.

And he has proven it with his performance as a City Councilman. But he felt compelled to become involved with, and put his name on, this effort.

Long Beach has earned its reputation as a culturally diverse and (for the most part) tolerant city. This new policy aboard the Queen Mary (which is, ultimately, owned by the city) is a continuation and strengthening of that reputation.

That's a good thing, an important thing.

And that makes it news.

20 YEARS OF SALT

I QUITE DELIBERATELY bared my soul in many "A Pinch," determined to make readers understand that there are really people behind the newspapers they read. Occasionally, I found myself talking through issues when someone accused me of less than stellar motives.

This was one such case. I had just convinced the City Council to more than double their financial commitment to the arts, and truly was worried about why I was so pleased.

August 23, 2001

Let's talk motivation. What motivates you to do what you do? What motivates that other guy or gal to do what he or she does?

For the purpose of this discussion, I'd like to limit the "do" to public affairs. Motivation in personal and family matters is an entirely different breed of cat – one better left to pastors and moralists to discuss.

What I'm talking about here is the motivation of public servants and community activists. The reason I'm talking about it is that I've had cause to question motives – mostly my own – in recent days.

You see, I've become a bit of an activist myself. That can be an uncomfortable position when you're a journalist by trade, but that's another story.

While I've become involved in several causes, support of the arts in Long Beach has been the one that has consumed me for the last few years. As chair of the Public Corporation for the Arts board, I've found myself in the position of advocate.

I've advocated increased public support of the arts in a variety of ways. I've asked other people for money and favors – something I hate to do – for the arts.

I think the arts community has made some progress.

But what has my motivation been? I spent most of last night mulling that question over.

I'd like to think I've been doing it for the good of the community. I believe in the importance of art and culture in a society. It is the soul of a community – the thing that makes life as a human being something more than survival.

But I have to ask myself, how much of what I'm doing is designed to give me increased standing in the community? How much personal pride is involved in deciding what to do?

I want to make sure I'm doing the right thing for the right reasons.

In my newspaper guy persona, one of the things I'm expected to do is consider people's motivations. Is a politician promoting a program for the good of the community, or for his or her own political advancement? Is a public servant doing a job a certain way because it's the right way or because it offers some personal gain?

Are activists opposing a project because they think it's wrong, or because they are seeking revenge against the proponents? Is an organization leader going his or her own way instead of working as a coalition because there is no common interest, or because they just don't like the other guys or girls?

I honestly believe that those of us involved in Long Beach are motivated mainly by the desire to make our city a better place to live. That goes for our politicians and our city employees. It also goes for those nay-saying activists I get so frustrated with.

If everyone would take a second to see some of that motivation, it might be a little easier to work with each other. It certainly is more productive than assigning the almost Satanic motivations our activists so readily (and falsely) attach to our city leaders.

It's foolish to ignore the personal motivations, though. Of course politicians are looking for issues to further their cause. Of course the activists want to feel the satisfaction of power over the process. Of course I want to make a difference, and have people know I did.

It's called being human. The trick is to make that the secondary motivation, not the primary one.

Do the right thing, for the right reasons. That's a decent rule to live by.

TECHNOLOGY HAS BEEN the boon and bane of the modern world. Nowhere is that more evident than with medical technology, where we routinely handle conditions that once were death sentences, lengthening lives. Those same technologies, though, can mean an existence as a vegetable, or great pain or as a helpless individual dependent on others.

A living will is one way to allow a small measure of control over that.

February 14, 2002

I got a letter from Dad the other day. It was one sentence. One thing is for sure – I didn't get my writing gene from him. Here it is, in its entirety:

"Here is the latest update to my living will. Love, Dad"

Dad is a hale and hearty 73. He plays golf three or four times a week (and usually beats me), takes care of his wife and mother and generally lives a good life.

He's been blessed with good health, and there is nothing on the horizon to make me think I'm going to have to make any life or death decisions for him. So there shouldn't have been a sinking feeling when I read that line, right?

Actually, after I got over the shock of opening the letter, I was proud of my father. He has determined that he doesn't want to "hang on" when his time comes, and he's taken steps to make sure that doesn't happen. It's a gift to us, too.

For those of you unfamiliar with a living will, the concept is fairly simple. It is a legal document providing guidelines of how a person wants to be treated should they be deathly ill and unable to speak for themselves. It tells doctors and loved ones when the individual wants them to "pull the plug," to put it crudely.

The idea is to avoid prolonging the inevitable beyond the reasonable expectation of recovery. The motive is to end the pain – for both the patient and his or her loved ones.

What's tough about a living will is the fact that you have to do it while you're living. Each and every one of us would rather think about the tennis match that night or even how to pay the bills than to consider what we want done if we're on the precipice of death.

Sadly, we here at the Gazette are experiencing what happens when that step isn't taken, though. Our beloved receptionist, Karen Thomason, is lying in a "rehabilitation hospital" right now. She is in what doctors call a vegetative state.

Almost exactly two months ago, Karen suffered a heart attack, a cerebral hemorrhage, then a series of strokes. Doctors did what doctors do, performing some medical miracles that kept Karen alive. There was hope that she would recover, if not fully, at least to the point where she would be able to enjoy life again.

It didn't happen. The doctors refuse to say Karen is in a coma, because she opens her eyes and her body "wakes up." But her mind is still asleep, at least as far as anyone can tell. There doesn't seem to be anyone behind those bright blue eyes.

Of course, there's always hope. God does perform miracles, and people have been known to recover from comas much longer than Karen's. We continue to pray.

But I don't think Karen would have wanted it this way. The woman who wouldn't even accept a ride home would be mortified to have people and machines caring for her bodily functions.

I'm no Angel of Death, and I certainly don't want to take responsibility for deciding someone else's fate. I say again, miracles do happen and maybe God has one in store for Karen – and us.

There aren't many plugs left to pull for Karen. Her body has stabilized, and short of stopping the food that goes through the tube or squeezing the air passage, there's not much anyone can do even if they, or Karen, wanted to resolve the situation.

With a living will, Karen would have had some control over the situation. She was just 51 years old when she was stricken. That's not exactly an age when you normally think about your death, let alone write a living will.

But maybe it should be.

THE SPIRIT OF FAITH

WHEN WE'RE CHILDREN, defining right and wrong seems pretty simple. But that black and white world quickly starts turning gray – or adding colors, if you prefer. When it comes to public policy, deciding what is the right thing is what politics is all about.

And I never let a chance to combine public policy and personal situations go to waste. But you have to read to the end to understand that.

August 1, 2002

Do the right thing. Sounds simple, doesn't it? As used in Jerry Vicich's cartoon above, it seems pretty straightforward. Do what you're supposed to do. Be ethical. Do the right thing.

I've said before that I believe our city leaders, be they elected or hired, do what they believe is best for the entire city virtually all the time. Despite more than 25 years in the newspaper business, I'm not much on conspiracy theories or nefarious, selfish motives.

Sure, there are some of those bad guys out there, and they should be ferreted out. But blaming every miscue, failed plan or service shortcoming on some sinister motive is too cynical a view of human nature, even for me.

They are trying to do the right thing. So why does it happen so often that it comes out wrong?

Because the devil is in the details. Take that literally.

The biggest question – what exactly is the right thing? When it comes to public policy, that's no easy question to answer. My idea of the right thing and your idea of the right thing can quite often be miles apart.

The hardest part is, that doesn't mean either my idea or your idea is wrong. For example, protecting residents near the airport from air and noise pollution is a right thing. But providing for the greater good of the city with a viable, thriving airport is a right thing, too. So what are you going to do?

In a democratic society, you try to provide a balance. Sadly, in this day and age, a judge in a court somewhere likely will decide what that balance is going to be.

Then there's how to do the right thing. In the public arena, the how quite often is the larger part of the debate. Do you build a movie complex or an amusement park? Do you finance through fees or borrow more money? Is there a "right thing" to do?

I don't pretend to have the answer. At some point, the powers that be must choose a path and, to use another cliché, just do it.

I do have a suggestion about how to prepare to do the right thing in the public arena, though. That is to try to do the right thing in your own life.

Of course, most of the same problems apply. What really is the right thing?

In my own life, I'm currently facing a pretty life-changing decision. A small child is involved. Superficially, the right thing is apparent – take care of the child. That's what good people do.

But if I do that, who else am I hurting? By "saving" one life, am I messing up half a dozen others?

What is the right thing to do? How do I decide?

Experience helps, and I'm gradually gathering quite a bit of that. Ironically, I think the times where I've done the wrong thing have taught me more.

Seeking advice helps too. It can really multiply that experience factor.

Personally, I've been turning to God, particularly on this latest issue. I don't expect to come across a burning bush any time soon, but I have found that if I let it happen, I get gentle nudges in the right direction. I just have to let myself be nudged.

So what am I, what are you, going to do? The right thing, of course.

As soon as we figure out what it is.

THE SPIRIT OF FAITH

THIS TRIP SOUTH of the border to build a home for a needy family has been one of, perhaps the, most powerful single experience of my Christian life. There was no way I could not write this column.

It was well received.

Oct. 9, 2003

I have been humbled.

Last weekend, Maria (my wife), John (my stepson) and I accompanied a group from Grace Community Church of Seal Beach (my church) to Mexico. We were there to build a home as part of something called Baja Christian Ministries, sort of a Habitat for Humanity south of the border.

There were about 40 of us. We stayed at a place near Tecate and drove about 20 miles to the hills surrounding Tijuana to our building site.

This is not the Mexico of Cabo, or even Ensenada. This is the real thing. The rutted road up the hill to the work site passed 8x10 shacks housing families of five or more, with no running water and single light bulbs powered by narrow strands of wire hanging from bare power lines.

And the people were smiling.

Just last week, I was cursing the cable television company for charging so much, and trying to figure out how to afford a trip to play some golf. I have been humbled.

When we arrived at 8 a .m. Saturday morning, there was a bare 16'x20' foundation and a tarp covering a bunch of lumber. When we left at 4 p.m. Sunday, there was a 400-square-foot, three-rooms-plus-a-loft home, painted on the outside and sheetrocked inside, with a locking door, four light fixtures, three outlets and a new outhouse out back.

In more than three years, I still haven't finished painting the inside of my house. I was humbled.

When we stopped for lunch and the neighbors came calling, I watched people stand in line for an hour, and then thank cooks with a tear in their eye for some potato salad and a piece of chicken. And I get impatient if my Sourdough Jack takes more than a minute. I was humbled.

I managed to do another of my klutz pratfalls, this time sliding off a roof to fall eight feet or so onto a ladder and sundry other construction equipment. I was working again an hour later with nothing more than a jammed wrist and plenty of bruises. It was one of the smaller miracles of the weekend. I was humbled.

I saw the overwhelming gratitude and pride of Ramon and Sophia as they held up the key to their new home. Ramon works longer hours than I do driving a taxi to bring home $50 to $70 a week, and the land (if you can call it that) his home is on will cost him $50 a month for the next four years. All he could say was that he didn't deserve our kindness.

I was humbled.

I watched as one person after another in our group stepped forward to lead in whatever capacity was necessary. I wasn't one of them. I was a follower. I was humbled.

I left California on Friday evening with 40 relative strangers. I returned Sunday with 40 brothers and sisters whom I can call friends and to whom I firmly believe I can turn to in times of need. I have a connection to a family in the near-Tijuana barrio. I have memories of working selflessly with my stepson and my wife for someone else's benefit.

I am humbled. And exalted. Thank you.

THE SPIRIT OF FAITH

TAKING CHRIST OUT of Christmas bothered many even before I became a committed, publicly confessing Christian. I couldn't very well leave it alone when I had the chance to publish on Christmas Day.

Dec. 25, 2003

Merry Christmas.

I know, we're not supposed to say that. It's not politically correct any more. Now it is supposed to be Happy Holidays.

There can't be any Christmas in our schools, although it's apparently okay to talk about Kwanzaa (I'm not sure how Hanukah stands). I'll bet the science classes discuss the winter solstice, but probably not in the Wiccan sense.

I do know the kids' time off is now "Winter Holiday," not Christmas Vacation.

Essentially every newspaper in the land is chock-full of Christmas stuff today, and ours is no exception. Christmas sales, Christmas dinners, Christmas charities. Santa Claus is everywhere.

Our good friend Jacques Warshauer and his dog Charlie try for the 24th consecutive year to explain the meaning of Christmas in his column, and they even have the temerity to name Jesus. My all-time favorite Christmas special on TV, "A Charlie Brown Christmas," uses a passage from the gospel of Luke as its centerpiece, although I don't recall Jesus being named specifically.

I hate the Xmas abbreviation. It is the ultimate secularization of Christmas — even worse than the huge merchandising push this time of year. It feels deliberately malicious to me.

Bottom line, Christmas is a religious holiday, and it is a Christian holiday. It began as a way to celebrate the birth of Jesus Christ - the sacrifice of God become man.

That said, I would be the last person to complain that non-Christians or non-practicing Christians participate in Christmas.

I'm thrilled to see the softening of hearts at this time of year, the Scrooges turned Samaritans, if only for a little while.

I get a kick out of the fact that those who get into "the Christmas spirit" are actually getting into a Christian spirit, even if they don't know it. A basic tenant of Jesus's teaching was the Golden Rule – love thy neighbor as thyself. What better definition of the Christmas spirit could there be?

In today's hectic, self-centered world, anything that makes us think of the other person first has to be a good thing. Christmas does that for many, both Christian and non-Christian.

Peace on earth, good will towards men is a sentiment that's hard to argue against. It seems particularly appropriate this year, what with Iraq, Afghanistan and the war on terrorism.

It's also true that Christians have no monopoly on that sentiment. That phrase applies to all men and women, regardless of faith or lack thereof.

I'm going to stick with Merry Christmas as my holiday greeting, because it reminds me of what I believe the holiday is all about. But when I say it, I'm not trying to be politically incorrect or proselytizing.

I'm sincerely wishing and hoping that you find the joy and meaning of this season. For you and yours, I hope for the best.

Merry Christmas to all.

THE SPIRIT OF FAITH

FINDING SOMETHING, OR more accurately, someone, to believe in seems to get harder every day. The ever-present and ever-growing corps of media and media wannabes work so hard to tear people down it is a wonder that anyone is left standing.

It seemed to me to be particularly bad early in 2004.

March 11, 2004

Once upon a time, I thought I wanted to be a hero. When I was a kid, I couldn't decide between Superman, Mickey Mantle or John F. Kennedy, but I knew I wanted to be some kind of hero.

I don't think I want to be a hero today. I've seen what we do to them.

Okay, Martha Stewart and Michael Eisner probably deserve to get slapped around a little for their rich arrogance. I've never been a huge Barry Bonds fan, Kobe should have known better and I cringe when I look at Michael (or Janet) Jackson.

But I feel bad when I watch Jason Giambi getting trashed, even if he shouldn't have taken the pump-me-up drug. I sigh when I watch Joe Namath make a drunken ass of himself on national television – over and over again, as the networks gleefully replay the debacle. I'm no Howard Dean supporter, but did we really have to drill him into the ground for one big squeal?

It appears that we do. At least, there certainly is a market for hero trashing. That's what all those grocery store tabloids are all about.

I think it's probably natural to want to see that our heroes are humans just like us. There's nothing wrong with realizing that the president has to use a bathroom or that a beauty queen has trouble with acne.

I just wish that we wouldn't express such glee when our heroes stumble.

It is, I think, our way of bringing them back down to our level. It becomes the great equalizer. So-and-so may be more talented, more good-looking, more rich or just more lucky than I.

But, as the cliché goes, the bigger they are, the harder they fall. And we love it when they fall.

These days, Superman is torn by teen-aged angst as well as being laid low by kryptonite. (The show's called "Smallville.") Mickey Mantle turns out to be a pill-popping boozer and Kennedy a pill-popping womanizer.

Those are the facts. That's supposed to make them closer to equal to me. It means, I guess, that my heroes are humans, too. So why doesn't that make me feel any better?

I think maybe I might still need some heroic heroes. Then maybe I can try to be closer to them.

I want to want to be a hero again.

THE SPIRIT OF FAITH

IF YOU HAVEN'T noticed by now, I have a bias against political correctness. It can get downright strident when people are politically correct at the expense of the expression of religion. The concern here wasn't really the county seal per se, but the step further down the road to acquiescing to the lowest common denominator.

June 24, 2004

I wanted to write an editorial last week about the absurdity of the controversy over the cross on the Los Angeles County seal. The American Civil Liberties Union (ACLU) threatened to sue if the cross was not removed and the county supervisors, at least enough of them, caved to the pressure.

I wanted this paper to editorialize about the unfairness of it all toward Christians and the Christian heritage of Los Angeles and California. I wanted to rail against the logic that allows a pagan goddess (Pomona, the goddess of fruit trees and gardens) to dominate the seal without challenge, but that demands removal of a miniature cross that is part of a mosaic that includes the Hollywood Bowl and the stars of television and movies, of all things.

But I didn't write the editorial about the county seal. Cooler heads on the editorial board prevailed. They said opinions about such things as religion belonged to individuals, not newspapers.

Well, I'm not so sure about that. But that's why we have an editorial board and not an editorial me.

It's also why I have this column.

Beyond the sad message this episode sends regarding our litigious society, I see it as an extreme swing of the pendulum regarding the separation of church and state. Somehow, the separation of church and state has become the elimination of church in the state.

When this country was formed, one of the fundamental principles, perhaps the fundamental principle, was freedom of religion (although a historian friend begs to differ). The whole concept of separation of church and state is designed to protect that freedom – government should not have the right to impose a particular religion.

But does acknowledgement of a religion equal imposition of that religion? I think not. Are we supposed to ignore the influence of Christianity on the development of our country, on California, on Los Angeles? That takes political correctness beyond the pale to ignore reality.

The concept is separation of church and state, not suppression of church by state. It doesn't matter if it is the liberal ACLU or the Stalinist Communists, suppression is wrong.

I don't want my government telling me what or how to worship. At the same time, I don't want my government to deny the influence of religion on our civilization.

Push the pendulum back to the middle, where it belongs. Or at least give me the address of the Church of Pomona, so I can sue them for putting their goddess on my county's seal.

THE SPIRIT OF FAITH

THIS WAS MY second trip to Mexico with members of my church. I felt compelled, again, to share the experience. This time, though, I tried to focus more on the people we helped than on how it impacted me.

I think it was just as powerful, if not more powerful than, the first experience.

Oct. 7, 2004

Have I mentioned lately how lucky I am, how blessed my life is? I got reminded again last weekend. It was in a place called Vista del Valle.

The view of the valley was indeed impressive after we had driven up the rutted dirt road. We could literally see for miles.

Vista del Valle is only about a four-hour drive from my Long Beach home. But it is a world away.

When stepson John and I (along with 60-some of our closest friends from Grace Community Church) got out of the car, our view of the valley was over literally thousands of shacks. Some were made of garage doors, others of reconstituted fiberboard or plywood.

Those shacks were, at most, 8 feet by 10 feet, with no windows and blankets for doors. When the blanket moved in the shack we stopped in front of, a weary woman followed by four boys emerged. A baby cried inside.

This was grandma, who had "inherited" the children. The mother was nowhere to be found, and we never saw a man on the site.

Further up the hill, another contingent from our church stopped in front of another shack. Out came a young woman, clearly no older than 18. She was about eight months pregnant, and a toddler wandered around nearby.

We were there to build these women houses. The hillside at Vista del Valle is filling up with these homes as Baja Christian

Ministries and other humanitarian groups try to improve the lives of the people there.

We built two homes in two days. Even given the fact that we had some incredibly talented builders (not me) in our group, that fact should give you some idea of the types of houses we are talking about. There is a 12-foot by 20-foot concrete foundation. There are three rooms (no doors between rooms) plus a sleeping loft.

We build an outhouse, but there is no running water. A barrel outside holds what is necessary to flush – make that rinse – the toilet.

There is some electricity – the connection is a bare wire looped across a cable strung on concrete poles – and we wire the home. There are three light fixtures in the entire building.

As I nailed the last bits of painted wood onto the front of the house to form a cross, the grandma looked up and smiled. One of the boys kept opening and closing the door, as if he wasn't sure the doorknob I had installed would really work.

The wonder and joy in their eyes was all the thanks we – our church we – needed or wanted. We had been blessed by helping.

Four hours later, we were back home. John looked in the refrigerator for something to drink. The television was on and the shower was waiting. I turned the light off in John's room as I went to my own room to read.

Have I mentioned lately how blessed my life is, how lucky I am?

THE SPIRIT OF FAITH

OCCASIONALLY, I'VE TRIED to use "A Pinch" to rally the troops, to try to motivate an action. I made use of my bully pulpit for several of my causes or charities that convinced me they were worthwhile.

This column was a plea to get involved while we still had a community to get involved with.

Aug. 4, 2005

I hope it is just that I'm getting older. I pray that it is just a phase, maybe the summer heat, causing it.

But I know that I am concerned, even afraid, as I watch violence escalate in our fair city, our country, our world. What's worse is that I'm not sure what to do about it.

I'd love to make light of the situation, to talk about all the potholes in the path to perdition (I've always wanted to say that).

But I can't. Too many lives are being ruined, either directly or indirectly.

It is depressing. As I drive to work each morning, I note that graffiti is proliferating. This summer's graffiti of choice appears to be elaborate, even artistic, defacing of billboards. I admit to a bit of guilty pleasure seeing these huge canvases being used creatively, but I bring myself up short when I realize it is a sign of the times — a bad sign.

That same graffiti is showing up on walls, median barriers, underpasses — just about everywhere. Another sad sign of the times is the number of freshly patch-painted walls, where owners have covered graffiti, with fresh signs, tags and "art" already in place. It has become a game.

That game is bad enough, but it is indicative of something worse. That's what waits for me virtually every day at the office.

"Thirty in fight, drive-by shooters arrested" one press release says. "One dead in shooting during fight" announces the press release the next day. "Man gunned down at noon" says the third day's police notice.

As Randy Newman says, "It's A Jungle Out There." And this is no song or television show.

I try to calm myself by saying I'm just noticing it more these days – that there were plenty of fights, graffiti and the like when I was a youngster, too. But even allowing for the "good old days" effect of rose-colored hindsight (I've always wanted to say that, too), there's no denying the violence is getting worse and more frequent.

What can I do? I'm not one to sit around and moan. I'd rather take action, no matter how feeble.

That's why I serve on the Parks and Recreation Commission, and why I agreed to become a board member at Goodwill of Greater Long Beach. It's why I didn't turn down an invitation to be a part of the steering committee for the 10-year plan to end homelessness in Long Beach. It's why my wife complains that I'm always at meetings instead of at home.

I don't pretend to understand the psyche of today's youth and the gang-bangers who seem to be responsible for so much of this fear and violence. But doing something is better than doing nothing. I turned to the experts to tell me how I could help, and they said, "Get involved."

It would be all too easy to retreat behind locked doors and barred windows. It would even be easy to leave the city and head for the hills – an option more and more are taking.

But if I do that, I'm admitting that the bad guys won. And I'm not ready to give up quite that easily.

So I got involved. Recreation programs, job programs, literacy programs, libraries, art programs – all have my support. I'll do what I can.

Want to help? I hope so. It's your city, too.

THE SPIRIT OF FAITH

FOR A GOOD chunk of my adult life, I subscribed to the "Be Here Now" theory of life I still have the book by that name by Baba Ram Das, for you old-time hippies. But with age comes a little maturity, and hopefully, a little perspective.

I still try to be here now, but with a little realization of what got me here now.

Dec. 29, 2005

Once upon a time, I would get excited as New Year's Eve approached.

It wasn't that I was a big partier (I was, but not on New Year's Eve). Rather I enjoyed the concept of a New Year – a fresh start, if you will.

I've written more than one column on the concept of Tabula Rasa, the blank slate. I would argue that the new beginning of a New Year worked best if we were able to set aside all the bad of the past. The whole concept of resolutions is to resolve to be new in the way we do things, isn't it?

But as I grow older, the weight of experience (and too many good meals) makes it harder to truly start over. The things I have done are harder to erase than the gray in my beard.

I seem to be less interested in erasing those things, as well. Maybe I've finally, after literally decades of trying, learned how to learn from at least some of my mistakes.

The slate never really goes blank – life isn't an Etch-a-Sketch we can shake to start over. And I've come to believe that that's not necessarily a bad thing – even when bad things are left on the screen.

Having teenagers and young adults at home reminds me how easy it is to know everything. I was that way once, if I remember correctly and what my dad says is true (the memory goes as the experience compounds).

It's undoubtedly true that I value experience more now than

I did 30 or 40 years ago largely because I have some now. The trick, I think, is what you do with that experience.

Over the last few months, I've been fascinated by a series National Public Radio has revived called "This I Believe," a series of essays from both the great and the obscure about — you guessed it — things people believe are important in their lives. While the beliefs cover the depth and breadth of human experience, they all seem to have one thing in common. The beliefs are based on experience.

This is what I believe — that you have to live every day as if it was your last. That doesn't necessarily mean partying New Year's Eve away, by the way.

It means doing the best you can at that moment, bringing all your experience to bear. It means learning from the mistakes you made, and building on your successes, not vice versa.

It means understanding you are forgiven, and forgiving others in the same way. It means teaching by example, and loving by action, not counting on words for either.

While my tabula isn't rasa, this is the first day of the rest of my life. I believe I can, and will, make it a good day, and a good year.

May you do the same.

Happy New Year.

THE SPIRIT OF FAITH

IT IS DIFFICULT to believe that we continue to watch the Muslim world explode in violence against the U.S. and its allies over perceived slights to their religion. It has become more and more obvious that the slights are being used as an excuse for what the hatred makes them want to do anyway.

When the fatwah was decreed against an editorial cartoonist, though, I couldn't help but talk about it and the concept of freedom of speech.

Feb. 16, 2006

I don't suppose either the Police Officers Association or its president, Steve James, are going to be too thrilled with today's editorial cartoon.

But I am virtually certain that I don't have to worry about a mob of angry cops attempting to burn down the Gazette Newspapers offices, or offering a reward for whacking cartoonist Jerry Vicich or Executive Editor Harry Saltzgaver (wait, that's me!) upside the head. I guess we should be happy neither James nor ex-Councilman Dan Baker is Muslim – at least I don't think they are.

I was sorry when I heard there were protests about a newspaper publishing a cartoon that had the temerity to show Mohammed in a less-than-flattering light. I have to admit I wasn't aware of the prohibition against images of the prophet of Moslem, but I also have to say that a Mohammed wearing a bomb-turban seemed to me to be a fair political comment given the situation in the Middle East.

I am flabbergasted that the whole thing has turned violent. Apparently governments that didn't slap down those nasty journalists (Danes are known to be a particularly insidious breed of rabble rousers) weren't showing enough respect for Muslim sensibilities, and deserved to have their embassies burned. People have died in violence over a cartoon that ostensibly has besmirched the honor of those following Mohammed.

People throwing firebombs because their prophet is depicted with a bomb – what am I missing here?

I was dismayed when "cooler heads" said publication of the cartoons should not have been allowed, that their very existence showed intolerance and disrespect. Since when has there been tolerance for Christian belief, let alone women's rights or – heaven forbid – gay rights in Iraq, Iran or the rest of the Muslim world?

This call of "can't we all just get along" is specious. There is no excuse for tolerating or explaining away violence in the name of protecting a religion's "honor."

Let's put the shoe on the other foot. I've seen plenty of American flags burned in the last four decades – it was downright popular in the 1960s and '70s. There were lots of patriots ready and willing to bash the heads of those flag burners. But that rarely happened, and when it did, the bashers were condemned and prosecuted.

When Robert Maplethorpe offered up a crucifix – Christ on the cross - in a jar of urine and called it art, his work was decried and even banned in some museums. But Christian radicals did not burn down the Cincinnati Museum of Modern Art, and the artist died a peaceful death, with no Crusaders (yes, I remember them) at his door.

Tolerance is important in this world. But being tolerant of intolerance is absurd, and being tolerant of violence is unacceptable. Isn't that what the cartoon was about in the first place?

THE SPIRIT OF FAITH

IT IS HARD to imagine how one could do more damage to Christianity than the lengthy series of sexual abuse cases in the Catholic Church. As bad as the violations by priests were, the cover-ups engaged in by church leadership were worse.

The scandal hit home in 2007, when the Archdiocese of Los Angeles agreed to a huge settlement rather than go through a case-by-case disaster.

July 19, 2007

> Trust.
> It's a simple word. Yet it's more valuable than gold.
> It's a little word – five small letters. It's easy to lose.
> The news this week is full of a $660 million settlement made by the Catholic Archdiocese of Los Angeles with 508 victims of alleged sexual abuse by members of the priesthood. The settlement, analysts say, was made to forestall punitive damages that could have been levied if the cases went to trial.
> Six hundred and sixty million dollars is a lot of money. Insurance claims will be filed and property sold to pay the bill.
> But that's not the most important thing the archdiocese – and to a large extent, the priesthood around the country – has lost. You know what the most important thing is, but I'll say it anyway.
> Trust.
> The most important thing a person can give another person is trust. Add the component of a person's spiritual well-being, and that trust elevates to the level of sacred.
> Sadly, stories of sexual abuse – to minors, to women, even to men – are less than scarce in our society. But the ongoing saga of abuse by religious leaders continues to appall. Why?
> Violation of sacred trust.
> No matter whether the person is a Catholic priest, a Protestant pastor or a Jewish rabbi, those in positions of religious responsibility come with a predisposition of trust – we expect their training

and screening to make them trustworthy.

In the course of most religious interactions, people are wont to share their innermost hopes and fears. That's true of all religions, although the Catholic emphasis on confession to and intercession by priests makes the expectation of trustworthiness even more important.

Loss of sacred trust is by no means reserved to the Catholic faith (although, as has been the case from time immemorial, the cover-up has only made matters worse). Televangelists, officials high in the hierarchy of various denominations and professing religious politicians all have managed to tar themselves and their peers by breaching the faith entrusted to them.

And that guilt by association is perhaps the worst consequence of all. Priests, pastors and the rest who abuse their position are miniscule in number compared to those faithfully fulfilling their calling. Yet, thanks to the actions of the abusers (and those covering up that abuse), the populace is much more skeptical of the clergy as a whole and the entire religious community.

It takes time to build trust, no matter what the forum. We don't trust doctors until we have some history with them. Ditto for lawyers, mechanics, bankers, even newspapers.

Yet that lengthy process of trust building can be undone with a moment's thoughtless action. The abuser not only has irreparably harmed the one abused, but the entire effort of bringing people closer to God.

I abhor all abuse – I can't even get my mind around the concept of finding some sort of pleasure in sexually molesting a child or forcing a woman to do something. Given my druthers, I would hang proven molesters by their – well, you know – instead of simply jailing them.

But setting back what many see as a divine task by the selfish act of personal gratification seems to me to be an even worse crime. Just as I get angry at "journalists" promoting their own agenda at the expense of honest reporting, thereby limiting my own credibility, I get angry at anyone in a position of trust violating that trust.

It is (yes, I'll use the word) a sin.

PUBLIC EXPRESSIONS OF faith have been controversial for decades. The ebb and flow has ebbed in recent years, particularly in California. The preferred path in recent years has been to err on the side of political correctness. So a political statement about religious freedom deserved a column of its own.

Jan. 17, 2008

Religion was mentioned Tuesday at the Long Beach City Council meeting.

It has been too long since that has happened. A few years ago, after protests from ACLU types and what I believe to have been an over-abundance of caution, the traditional invocation to open council meetings was replaced by "a moment of silence to contemplate."

That invocation had been offered by everyone from Baptist ministers to Buddhist monks. I even recall at least one Native American shaman, although I must admit that I don't remember the last time I saw a Muslim Imam standing before the council.

Elimination of the invocation took place quietly — no protests, no banner headlines. It just sort of happened.

That's sad. At the risk of sounding flip and not meaning to, our city leaders can use every bit of help they can get. That's true of every leader in our country, no, our world.

Some apparently felt uncomfortable about a public prayer, no matter who was doing the praying. So be it.

But don't expect religion to go away. My pastor, Don Shoemaker, certainly doesn't.

A longtime Long Beach resident, Shoemaker is senior pastor at Grace Community Church in Seal Beach. He long has been active in area and national religious organizations, and has never hesitated to make his opinion known, particularly when it comes to the freedom to worship.

His pet peeve is the fact the Long Beach Marathon is run on a

THE SPIRIT OF FAITH

Sunday, and blocks roads people normally use to get to churches. But that is fodder for another column.

Shoemaker is nothing if not proactive. This time around, he took the ball of Religious Freedom Day and ran with it.

As every schoolchild knows, religious freedom was one of, maybe the, founding principles of this nation. For some time, that freedom has been emphasized as a freedom from religion in government affairs. The other side of the coin has, in my opinion, been given short shrift.

But back to the story. Shoemaker had noticed that the federal government had begun (in 1994) to mark Jan. 16 as Religious Freedom Day. The date is the anniversary of the Virginia Statute for Religious Freedom, passed on Jan. 16, 1786.

So he formed a committee and drafted a proclamation that would make Jan. 16 Religious Freedom Day in Long Beach. Note that it does not say Religious Day. To quote the proclamation:

"Our country has embraced a tradition of religious liberty – where people have been left free to choose which faith they shall follow or none at all."

Shoemaker garnered support from both conservative and liberal religious leaders for his proclamation. Then he went to his council representative, Fifth District Councilwoman Gerrie Schipske, and got it on the Jan. 15 agenda.

I have no clue what Schipske's spiritual walk is, nor do I want to know. I give her credit for recognizing a basic American right and moving it forward in Long Beach.

Bottom line for me: I'm not asking everyone to pray with me, I'm just asking for the right to pray. I think Pastor Shoemaker made that a little easier this week, and for that I'm thankful.

Now you can have that moment of silence from me.

20 YEARS OF SALT

FALSE PROPHETS HAVE been misleading people for eons. In fact, figuring out who is a true prophet has plagued man for those same eons. It's why, I think, it takes faith to become a Christian.

False prophets like Camping cost people their livelihoods, sometimes their lives. I attempt to offer an alternative here.

May 19, 2010

Are you still here?

Let's check again on Saturday. If you're still here then, you might be in trouble.

At least that's the intimation from a postcard I received this week. According to a guy named Harold Camping, the end of the world is/was Friday, May 21.

So how could you be here Saturday if the world has ended? Well, according to the postcard, the world only ends for those who have been saved, and who will be raptured that day. For the unsaved, there will be five months of shame and torture before they are snuffed out.

And we wonder why it's so hard to be a Christian these days.

Guys like Camping, who runs something called Family Radio and has a Worldwide Christian Ministry — his Web site says so — make it more than a little difficult to establish any credibility as a Christian. The only solace is that end-of-the-world prophecies have been around since, oh, the beginning of the world. So far, none have come true, as far as I know.

I have to admit to a bit of ambivalence here. My religion does indeed teach that the day will come when the world as we know it will cease to exist. It includes the notion of salvation.

So how can I make fun of Mr. Camping and his ilk? One of these days, one of these times, one of these guys is going to be right, if the Bible is to be believed.

Oh, before I forget, let me explain this rapture phenomenon. That's when the truly saved are supposed to be gathered to God, disappearing from this earthly plane (or is it plain?). If you remember the "Left Behind" series of books that were very popular a decade or so ago, such an instantaneous departure is going to make a bit of a mess. But in that scenario, at least those left behind had three and a half years to be saved before judgment day.

So what's a good Christian to do? You don't know when the test is going to be complete – when the ultimate Teacher is going to say "pencils down."

It turns out there's a pretty effective solution. Better yet, it works even if you don't happen to believe the world might end any time soon.

It's being the best you can be. Now.

Those of us of the Christian persuasion sometimes call it being right with God. We add a dash of belief to the basic mantra of being the best person you can be, but it comes down to the same thing.

You know, follow the Golden Rule, be righteous and charitable, that kind of stuff. I prefer the proactive of being and doing to the denial of a sin-based approach, but I'm just that kind of guy. After all, doing unto others as you would have them do unto you sort of precludes murder, doesn't it?

I saw a news story the other day about some outfit selling survival bunkers in the desert. There is another outfit marketing luxury underground condos in Kansas guaranteed to withstand the apocalypse in style.

But if the world ends, what are those developers going to do with all their money?

The end of the world gurus have plenty to work with these days – major earthquakes, frequent famines, wars around the world, now the gushing of the world's own blood fouling the oceans. Has it ever been worse? Have the signs ever been clearer?

Well, when I was growing up, people were turning their basements into bomb shelters in preparation for the imminent nuclear attack by the Soviet Union. We clearly were naïve – everyone knows you have to be 50 feet underground to survive the bomb. That basement stuff is for tornadoes.

I suspect much of Europe thought the world was ending during the Black Plague. What do you think the folks at the base of Pompeii thought?

You get my point.

Are you ready? Me neither.

But I'm doing my best to get that way.

THE SPIRIT OF FAITH

ONE OF THE greatest things about writing a column is the ability to escape journalistic integrity to offer an opinion. Another great thing is it offers a safe place for a little confession – at least if there's a good enough reason.

I thought this was a good enough reason.

Dec. 1, 2010

For more than a year now, I've managed to stay out of the medical marijuana debate, at least personally.

Of course, that doesn't mean the paper has ignored it. We've covered it as carefully, if not more so, than anyone else in the city. We've also offered editorial opinion on the issue, and I'll admit to having a little bit to do with that.

But I've never laid out how I personally feel about the issue. Well, I feel compelled today to come clean, if you'll pardon the pun.

The impetus for the spasm of unburdening comes from a story that ran on the front page of last week's Uptown Gazette about a couple of marijuana dispensaries in Bixby Knolls. Actually, it wasn't the story itself, in which Leslie Smith provided a nicely balanced look at the struggles of the city to regulate versus the cooperatives attempting to stay in business.

We've done similar stories about cooperatives on the east side of town. Some operators are willing, even anxious, to cooperate (pardon that pun, too) and get their story out while others – not so much. I've watched hours and hours of public debate and comment at City Council meetings exploring all sides of the issue, all without feeling compelled to talk pot in this column.

What really got me going was the debate the Bixby Knolls story spurred in the comment section of our website. Someone who I'm fairly certain would be proud to be called a staunch conservative took on a medical marijuana advocate who says he is a doctor and who believes the coops provide an important service. Go to www.gazettes.com to see the discussion and even join in if you like.

I don't get into the middle of those comment debates – that's a readers' forum. But it did convince me it was about time for me to come out from behind my shield of journalistic objectivity.

I'll start by saying that I'm of an age. I was in high school in the era of the Beatles, and missed going to Woodstock by about a year. I was in college in the love child days of the early 1970s.

I was a straight arrow in high school. Oh, I did the beer thing with my jock buddies after the games, but I stayed away from the demon weed.

Did I mention I was in college in the '70s? It was different, much different, than high school. And yes, I inhaled.

I survived that period somehow, with my brain mostly intact (feel free to disagree). I quit when I decided short-term memory was an attribute I needed to maintain to function. That was a few decades ago.

I was bemused when the idea of marijuana as medicine gained credence. I certainly could see how it would benefit appetite and I had no problem believing it helped in other ways.

But it was clear to me that the medical marijuana dispensaries that proliferated in California had only a passing concern with providing medicine. The sheer number of outlets made it clear this was an easy way to get something that was nominally illegal in a sort-of-legal way. And the "nonprofit" component of the deal clearly is a joke, at least in most cases.

So I should be coming down on the side of trying to regulate them out of existence, right? Until the country decides the weed should be legal, then it is illegal by definition, right?

But. And it is a big but for me. Let me take you to the Bible. Wait – don't stop reading. This is a story, not a religious lesson.

In Genesis 18, Abraham argues with God over the fate of Sodom. God wants to destroy the city because of the great evil there. But Abraham argues it should be saved for the sake of the few righteous people there. He bargains God down from 50 righteous people to just 10 righteous men.

Sadly, Sodom was still destroyed — there weren't even 10 righteous men. But I have to say that I believe Abraham's principle holds true for medical marijuana. Regulate if you must, but if it helps, truly helps, even one person handle pernicious diseases like cancer and AIDS, we have to continue to make it available.

Medical marijuana has a place in this world, and we have a duty to allow it to keep its place. Why? Because it is the right thing to do.

20 YEARS OF SALT

FOR A NUMBER of years now, I have started every day with this little prayer. As is often the case, trying to explain it to others has helped me understand it. Reading it again, I managed to understand a little more.

Jan. 6, 2011

I quit making New Year's resolutions several years ago – not because it's a bad thing to resolve to do better at something, but because I had a tendency toward unrealistic expectations.

You know what I mean. I'd promise myself to be out of debt by the end of the year, to lose 50 pounds, to not lose my temper, that sort of thing. As any pop psychologist will tell you, that's just setting yourself up for failure, and you can actually end up worse off than when you started.

Instead, I've been relying more and more on a little prayer I learned a long time ago.

It's called the Serenity Prayer, and was written by theologian Reinhold Niebuhr. The entire prayer is 14 or 16 lines long, depending on the place you get it from. But the famous version, the one hanging in homes and meeting halls across the world, is just four lines:

God, grant me the serenity/
To accept the things I cannot change/
The courage to change the things I can/
And the wisdom to know the difference.

As most people know, Alcoholics Anonymous has adopted the prayer as sort of a shorthand philosophy of life. The primary idea is that it offers the serenity necessary to live without resorting to alcohol or other escapes – to understand that there are things beyond our control.

If you are able to get past that first step (and it is a much bigger step than you might think at first glance), those last two lines offer a totally different challenge. They also turn the prayer – and

THE SPIRIT OF FAITH

the prayee, so to speak — around, from an attitude of passive acceptance to one of positive action.

I could write pages on my struggle with the first two lines; giving up control is not one of the things I do easily. But the new year is a time to talk about action, right?

Do I, or you, have the courage to change the things we have control over? I don't know about you, but I have a tendency to resist change. I know why, too. I learned it in my high school physics class (yes, they taught physics in the last century).

Put simply, it takes energy to put an object in motion, and the bigger the object, the more energy it takes. To move something as big as a lifestyle, an inordinate amount of energy is required.

On the other hand, it takes just a little energy to keep something moving once it is motion. In fact, stopping the motion is what really requires energy.

So it is little wonder that my first inclination is to accept the status quo. It takes less energy to just go along. And now I've got the excuse that it's (whatever it is) probably something I cannot change, so I should just accept it, right?

Wrong. That's why the full line asks for the courage to change the things I can. Another translation actually says to change the things which should be changed. There's a call to action here to make things better. You should do it, whether it is hard or not.

The real kicker, of course, is the last line. Just how do you decide what you can't change and what should be changed?

It takes wisdom — and wisdom is tough to come by, at least for me. I suppose that's why it is a prayer. I'm asking for something that I have little reason to expect should be mine.

Experience is one path to wisdom, and it is the one I'm most familiar with. I have hope that my experiences, in particular my mistakes, have given me a few guidelines in what I attempt to change.

Time will tell. For now, I'll keep praying.

TALK ABOUT THE apocalypse, the end of the world, the end times, seems to run in cycles. However, I suspect the end of the world becomes a hot topic at least once a generation. The popularity of the Left Behind series by Tim LaHaye and Jerry B. Jenkins brought the debate to into the mainstream, at least for a while.

I've been taught to not worry so much about the when and focus on whether I'm ready if. Some natural phenomena gave me the chance to talk about that.

Jan. 13, 2011

> The sky is falling, the sky is falling!
> Wait, that's not right. How about, the birds are falling, the birds are falling!
> I'm writing this on Day One. That's not the first day, but it is the day (or one of them) when the date is all ones – 1-11-11. Only Nov. 11 of this year will be more auspicious for all you numerologists out there.
> So it seems only fitting that I write (again) about the apocalypse.
> The latest round of concern began ratcheting up on New Year's Eve, when about 5,000 red-winged blackbirds fell from the Arkansas sky. At first, the arguments that it was a weird but natural phenomenon equaled claims of secret government experiments, which in turn equaled prophecies of the end of the world.
> But then entire flocks of different bird species (admittedly smaller flocks, but still) began falling from the sky in Louisiana, Kentucky and across Europe. It was reported this morning that a flock of more than 100 birds were found dead near the 101 north of Los Angeles, so it's getting closer.
> What is it? Well, that's what makes it all so interesting. No one seems to know, exactly.
> Some scientists claimed the Arkansas die-off was caused by fireworks or something similar – the birds were literally scared to death. Turns out that area residents had been trying to get the

flock to move for some time (mainly because of something else falling out of the sky), so there was motive.

But the end times prognosticators gained traction when the media began looking for, and finding, mass deaths in other places. Scientists tried to fight back with feeble claims of population balancing and coincidence. But most people had made up their minds.

It was the aflockalypse.

Does that mean the end of the world is at hand? Well, if those aforementioned scientists could link the various die-offs through some sort of environmental change, it certainly could be a precursor of the end of the world as we know it. Do you think the first birds who died of cold knew that the Ice Age was coming?

But at least as far as I know, that isn't the case. So is there a deeper spiritual meaning?

I won't go into all of the Biblical signs of the end times as found in the book of Revelation and elsewhere, but as far as I know, bird deaths isn't called out specifically. You might want to watch out for a third of the stars falling out of the sky, or all of your Christian friends disappearing, but until then …

We humans are desperately interested in knowing what's going to happen when, up to and including our own demise. Some think that knowledge would allow them to change the end result, while others think it would change the way people act now.

Whatever the reason, people have been trying to predict the end of the world for thousands of years. Even those believers who lived in Christ's time were guilty – a lot of them thought Jesus said it was going to happen in their lifetime.

When that didn't happen, the Nostradamus types began to surface. Everything from an eclipse to a super cold winter was cause to tell people to prepare their souls.

These days, we have the end of the Mayan calendar, the nuclear threat, global warming – plenty of reasons to believe the end is near. Disappearing bees and dying birds just add to the list.

Unless you happen to know when the alien spaceship arrives to save the last few humans, I have a hard time seeing how it matters. If you're waiting for the end-of-the-world date to start being a good person, I've got a little tip for you.

Your end of the world, my end of the world, could happen today. The Arizona shootings are just the latest example of how fleeting life is.

It kind of makes sense to be ready no matter when it happens, doesn't it? Easy to say, hard to do, I know. But I think it's a good idea to try.

And I don't want to wait until a bird falls on my head to do it.

THE SPIRIT OF FAITH

CALL IT A slippery slope, or the first step down a long path the wrong way. Actually, the slide down the slope, that first step, took place long ago, when society started working, playing golf, selling liquor on the Sabbath. That trip, that slide, made it easy to declare that Easter didn't qualify as a legal holiday.

It didn't make it right.

April 24, 2011

Did you know that Easter isn't a holiday?

At least it isn't a holiday when it comes to governments and banks. And up until 1 p.m. or so Tuesday, it isn't a holiday when it comes to parking meters.

That's right. Until there was a virtual uprising, the city was expecting you to bring some quarters if you had a nice Easter brunch planned on Second Street or downtown.

The brouhaha began last year, at least in the Shore, after it was decided to start expecting people to pay the meters on Sundays. That included Easter, the city thought. Ultimately, some poor parking meter guy was driving around with a bullhorn, trying to convince people they had to pay the meters. That just made it worse.

In the end, the city voided those tickets. And now the city attorney says no tickets will be written this Sunday.

But is Easter I real holiday?

It sure is a big deal in my house, and in most Christian households. (Let's just ignore that bunny movie shall we?) Ask a pastor or a priest, and you'll find it is equal to Christmas, maybe more important, at least when it comes to theology.

But no offices I know of take the Monday after Easter off. It's not part of the paid holiday schedule in any union agreement I'm aware of. Some folks take the Friday before off (Good Friday – try to explain to a youngster why the day Christ was crucified is called Good Friday), but that usually requires spending a vacation day.

I have a few theories. First, Easter is always on a Sunday. There's still that vestige from Puritan days when every Sunday is seen as a day off.

So why would you declare a day off when the banks are already closed?

As an aside, this is where the parking meter thing became problematic. For years, meters weren't enforced on Sunday, so there was no debate about whether Easter was a holiday or not. Then the city or somebody decided that it was important to get every last quarter, and the meters went live seven days a week. I predict that some day they'll decide to enforce them 24/7 via computer or something.

But back to the holiday issue. Perhaps Easter is too religious to be a society-wide holiday. It is, after all, a particularly Christian holiday. That's despite all the best efforts by the candy-making lobby (I told you to forget that movie, didn't I?).

Restaurateurs have joined the card makers and the candy sellers to capitalize on Easter, and I say more power to them. But it still isn't a legal holiday. Instead, it ranks along with Valentine's Day or Halloween, and that isn't a good thing, from my point of view.

Then again, maybe it would be better if we keep Easter to ourselves. It's tough enough to convince the 10-year-old in my life that the day is more about resurrection than chocolate bunnies and jellybeans. (Okay, so that movie played to common sensibilities. But can't we ignore it?)

I've written before about Easter as a symbol of renewal and of spring. I've managed to get myself in trouble with pagans and to totally mess up the relationship between Easter and the Jewish Passover.

So you'd think that I'd learn to leave well enough alone. But nope, I have to keep writing about Easter. Why, oh why, can't I leave it alone?

Why? Because the promise that is behind Easter is something

to celebrate. It is a central tenant in my belief system. In many ways, Easter is Christianity.

So whether I need to feed the parking meter or not, Easter is a holiday.

20 YEARS OF SALT

IN 2011, FOOTBALL player Tim Tebow became a phenomenon. Not necessarily because he was a great football player (the jury is still very far out on that), but because he wore his faith on his sleeve. During a fairly miraculous rookie season run, he had the temerity to kneel and thank God.

That made him a target for debate, even scorn. I didn't like that. Go figure.

Dec. 15, 2011

In the past, I've used this space to extol the thought-provoking virtues of KPCC, the all-talk National Public Radio (NPR) station based at Pasadena City College.

So I think, I hope, I'm within bounds to take issue with what I heard on that station on Monday. Patt Morrison, a weekly columnist for the Los Angeles Times, gets a full hour each weekday afternoon to explore issues, and she ranges far and wide.

This particular show, she decided to talk about how people felt when they saw athletes praising God. The immediate cause for the topic was Tim Tebow and the Denver Broncos, who have been on a winning streak of mythic proportions. The Broncos were behind the Bears 10-0 on Sunday with less than three minutes to go. They won the game 13-10 in overtime.

The Broncos have been behind virtually every game in the fourth quarter, have won three overtime games in a row and are 7-1 since Tebow became the starter. The Comeback Kid is completely inadequate in describing what he and the Broncos have accomplished.

But Morrison wasn't on the air to debate whether Tebow has the stuff to be an NFL quarterback (most "experts" still say no). She was there to talk about how Tebow, and some other players, wear their faith on their sleeve, thanking God, pointing to the sky, assuming postures of prayer, etc.

Her question, nay, her hypothesis, was that God had no place on the sporting field and these players were forcing God down unwilling people's throats.

Talk about feeding the stereotype of the faithless liberal press.

It didn't help any that her call screeners seemed intent on making sure that every caller who got on the air was an avowed atheist or someone saying that even if there is a God, he's certainly got more important things to do than to pay attention to a football game.

To give the devil her due, Morrison did air a clip of Bob Costas talking about how Tebow expresses his faith without claiming that God is on his side, or that He has any impact on the outcome of games. But the overriding assumption in the hour was that any athlete who invoked or thanked God must be praying for victory permeated both hers and her callers' comments.

They're simply wrong.

I'm not saying that every athlete is full of faith and that there are no hypocrites among those who point to the sky after a home run or take a knee after a touchdown. But I am saying that the player who thinks it through to the point where they are trying to proclaim that they are God's chosen are few and far between.

I'd like to suggest that the basic assumption – that players are praying for victory, or thanking God for victory – is wrong. If Morrison or her callers had ever been in a prayer circle before a game, they'd know better.

Prayers are for the ability to do your best. Prayers are for the strength to perform in a Christian manner, giving your all and respecting that your opponent is giving theirs.

What about Tebowing – assuming an attitude of prayer after a good play? Most Christians believe in giving praise and thanks to God at the end of something – most often for the simple fact that Christians believe that God is with them, allowing their very existence, as well as their performance.

The phrase is: "All praise to you, God," and the purpose is to remain humble in victory (or defeat).

It there a component of proselytizing in these displays of faith? Yes, I guess there is. These players want it known that they are believers in the hope that they will show that believers can be successful athletes, too.

Given the alternative of players who pound their chests, offer extravagant celebration dances and generally scream "see how great I am" every time they make a tackle or gain five yards, I'm pretty comfortable with a man saying, "oh, and I believe in God."

Keep humble, Tim Tebow. And keep winning.

Part SIX
One More For Good Measure

ONE MORE FOR GOOD MEASURE

AND HERE IT is – the column about being at Gazette Newspapers for 20 years. It is the end of the book, but doesn't appear to be the end of my career. I am thankful for that.

March 18, 2012

I wasn't going to write about it.

Honest, I planned on just letting it slide by. I really don't like milestone columns.

But the column I had planned, something about that devil incarnate (or is he just a clueless imbecile?) on talk radio, fell through when the person I needed to talk to fell victim to that nasty flu that's been going around.

It's past deadline, and I've got to do something. So here goes. Apologies in advance for those of you who don't care for milestones, either.

Twenty years ago last Friday (March 16), I became the executive editor of Gazette Newspapers.

In Lincolnesque terms, that's a score. Call it a generation.

There are a few editorial types in Long Beach who've been here longer than I have, but very few. I can count them on one hand, and refuse to embarrass them by name.

Twenty years ago, there was no such thing as email. We used computers to work, but telephones to communicate. It took 10 minutes to print a page – 15 if it had a picture on it.

Speaking of pictures, ours were all in black and white. We ran something called spot color to shade boxes or advertisements, but it was a point of pride for then owner and publisher John Blowitz that we were the last paper around to not print pictures in that expensive four-color process.

Ah, John and his wife and co-owner Fran (she really ran the show, at least in terms of the business end). We had some times. We agreed so completely in the philosophy of community newspapers that I was looking for an apartment here the day after I first interviewed.

It wasn't all sweetness and light, though. Far from it. Our battles were epic, usually ending with me pouting in one corner and John and/or Fran fuming in another.

Bet you didn't know that, did you? That's because we never let it show in the paper. We had the same goal, to put out the best publication in the city, and we wouldn't let anything get in the way of that, including our own feelings.

When I began, the Grunion Gazette struggled to 32 pages, with a 40-pager a milestone. I still remember the staff meeting when we vowed never to let the Downtown go below a 20 again.

We grew, and grew mightily. In the boom days, the Grunion regularly hit 80 pages. When Grand Prix time rolled around, we'd throw something on the porch with the heft of a Sunday Times.

I grew too. It wasn't easy – I pretty much knew everything there was to know when I got here, and growing into the realization that I didn't know so much after all proved painful.

It took a lot of forbearance from John and Fran, and a lot of support. I made some colossal mistakes – more personally than professionally, I think – and I appeared destined to learn only through severe pain. And thanks to this little column, I've done quite a bit of it in the glare of public awareness.

I've shared my joys – a son growing into a man, then a dad – and my pains. You, gentle reader, have been there for divorces, weddings, deaths and births.

I've found God and lost the compulsion for alcohol. I've suffered a heart attack, quit smoking and gained weight – all right here before your eyes.

I've ranted and raved about the foibles and follies of Long Beach, I've cajoled and pleaded for support of the arts, schools, charities and parks, and hopefully I've been generous with my praise and pride in the city and people I've come to love.

I've tried to keep up with the ever-increasing pace of change, from the technology of our information industry to the priorities of our city government. I've made sure that our Gazettes – now five with the addition www.gazettes.com, the Uptown Gazette and www.gazettessports.com – remained focused on serving our community, and I've tried to serve the community on my own as well.

It's been one hell of a ride. And it was a ride I wouldn't give back for anything.

I couldn't have done it without you, dear reader. After all, I have to have an audience, don't I?

I strongly doubt that I'm going to make it another 20 years. That's a long, long time. But I don't have any plans on leaving anytime soon, either.

So keep putting up with me, won't you? Thanks.

CPSIA information can be obtained at www.ICGtesting.com
Printed in the USA
BVOW000913290313

316806BV00004B/8/P